DESIGN FOR A LIMITED PLANET
LIVING WITH NATURAL ENERGY

Norma Skurka and Jon Naar

Ballantine Books • New York

All rights reserved under International and Pan-American
Copyright Conventions. Published in the United States by
Ballantine Books, a division of Random House, Inc., New York
and simultaneously in Canada by Ballantine Books of Canada,
Ltd., Toronto, Canada.

All photographs are by Jon Naar, except for the following pictures: page facing epigraph page © David
Plowden; page 28 © Harold Hay; pages 104 and 107 are
by Lee Porter Butler; pages 116 to 119 are by Ernest
McMullen. Diagrams are by architect and solar
consultant, Avi Maor.

Library of Congress Catalog Card Number: 76-9869

ISBN 0-345-27315-X

Manfactured in the United States of America

First Edition: November 1976
Second Printing: May 1977

Art direction by Ian Summers

Book design by Bryan Dew

Design for a Limited Planet
Living with Natural Energy

"...We do not own the freshness of the air and the sparkle of the water, how can you buy them from us? Every part of this earth is sacred to my people. Every shining pine needle, every sandy shore, every mist in the dark woods, every clearing and humming insect is holy in the memory and experience of my people. We know that the white man does not understand our ways. One portion of the land is the same to him as the next, for he is a stranger who comes in the night and takes what he needs. The earth is not his brother, but his enemy and when he has conquered it he moves on. He leaves his fathers' graves and his children's birthright is forgotten."

An excerpt from a letter sent to President Franklin Pierce from Indian Chief Seathl in the 1850s when the United States was purchasing the territory that is now the state of Washington.

Contents

Foreword   *by Jacques-Yves Cousteau*

The world was brutally introduced to the nuclear age. Instead of stealing fire from heaven, Prometheus had extracted it from the very heart of matter.

During the years that followed World War II, there was no doubt in my mind that once again progress born out of the horrors of war would be tamed for peaceful uses. Taming atomic bombs into atomic power was just a modern way to melt Roman swords into plowshares.

In 1959, as director of the Oceanographic Institute in Monaco, I hosted the first international conference on the disposal of nuclear waste. It was generally agreed that the quantities of nuclear waste to be produced in the future would be enormous. What to do with it was the hot issue. Listening to all the debates, my conclusions were:

First, the only participants who dared express doubts about the planned disposal operations did not belong to a nuclear agency or had nothing to gain from atomic proliferation.

Second, with few exceptions, the pros came from specialists in physics and chemistry, while the cons were expressed by biologists and physiologists. Finally, when the Russians violently opposed Western plans to dump wastes in the ocean, I realized that the issue was clouded by politics as well.

Simple, basic questions about actual efficiency, economic validity and safety remain unanswered after 17 years. Nuclear technology has formidable implications on the way the world has to be run. No other single enterprise touches all the issues of our time: the need to avoid nuclear war, and the corresponding need to provide a basis for justice and equity among the communities of our planet; the right of all people to lead healthy and fulfilling lives; our right to social structures founded on dignity and freedom; our relationship to the beautiful, intricate, fragile and increasingly imperiled world on whose survival our own depends; and, above all, the obligations we bear to our descendants.

We are able to carry on our "energy trip" only by *cheating*—either we burn in a few decades the fossil carbon accumulated over hundreds of millions of years, or we draw an atomic check on our descendants, endangering almost forever natural balances indispensable for the survival of mankind.

Since the war, we have entangled ourselves in a questionable energy option—the atomic cycle—and it will become more difficult and more costly to switch to other solutions with each passing year.

Today, however, the world energy policy is in transition. The nuclear commitments being contemplated now dwarf those made in the past. Thoughtful people throughout the world are pausing to re-examine the assumptions on which those commitments have been built with so little discussion.

Could we not also pause long enough to consider the feasibility, on an international scale, of developing renewable resources to meet the energy needs of all people in all nations? Would not the advancement of appropriate non-nuclear technologies be a better place to concentrate international effort than nuclear promotion, which already has such powerful private and national interests behind it?

Should we not take advantage of this chance to consider alternatives before plunging ahead with a nuclear policy that may well prove, on riper examination, to be mistaken or impracticable? Should we not take advantage of the possibility that radical changes in energy policy in a few countries, even in the United States alone, might remove the political support that now maintains nuclear momentum elsewhere? Might not the movement for a non-nuclear energy policy in the United States be translated into a strong international commitment to develop and make freely available those technologies that respect social and biological constraints?

It is long past time to recognize the proliferation of reactors and of bombs as two interwined aspects of the same problem; nonproliferation of reactors and reduction of strategic arms as two interwined solutions.

The toxic and explosive material produced in nuclear plants will have to be meticulously maintained for periods as long as tens of millions of years—far longer than any one human culture has ever lasted. This means that extremely high levels of dedication, vigilance and quality control must be maintained without interruption, indefinitely, a situation totally alien to the human condition. In other words, safe containment for future generations means all nations participating in the atomic venture will have to be ruled by stable governments, and maintain reliable police forces for millions of years!

Despite the best efforts and intentions of the people of the United Nations, human society is too diverse, national passions too strong, human aggressiveness too deep-seated, for the peaceful and the warlike atom to stay divorced for long. We cannot embrace one while abhorring the other; we must learn, if we want to live at all, to live without both.

—from an address delivered at the conference on nuclear energy and world order at the United Nations, May 1976.

When I presented the above thoughts to diplomats from nearly every government on our Water Planet, I was concerned that a diabolical situation facing future generations of our species be appropriately characterized in all its heinousness. The lethal debris from atomic power is a quiet violence we are perpetrating on our children and grandchildren. It may be the greatest danger we know about today, because it contaminates, not only the bodies of living things, but the political systems that will eventually arise to control its terrible potential.

But there are hopes, great hopes, and they are these: the creativity and the common sense of people like the men and women whose works are described here. If we must learn to speculate more about the degree of concern for life held by our governments and our industries, then we must concurrently begin to trust individual initiative and intelligence. The creative engines of the great social and business institutions reside in a few minds present at a few research and development meetings. In such isolation, there is the capacity for unrealistic decisions and mistakes which tend to be large mistakes. But thousands of free-thinking individuals, taking thousands of small random steps forward, risking their savings and investing their spare time, will make only small mistakes on the way to accumulating a large aggregate success. The automobile itself is a system developed part by part in widely-separated garages across decades by inspired individuals.

That is how humanity has developed the colossal technologies which, ironically, are so successful that they now threaten to engulf us. But that is also how we will save ourselves, if it is not too late, in the next fifty years: by modifying our own homes and lifestyles, improving the quality of our own lives, so that we are consuming only renewable energy, food and goods. To do otherwise is to rob our progeny. And it is one way of regaining a very important measure of control over our lives—independently producing most of the energy required by our dwellings.

What in the world makes more sense than solar power? It will last as long as life on earth, until the sun swells out to become a Red Giant and consumes us in about four billion years. It arrives free from the generating station. It does not spill or leak. It does nothing more to the airspaces above our cities than brighten them.

It is an obvious solution, and it will come about —because the people in this book have experimented boldly, because you who read it will improve on their work and your genius will in turn be questioned and remodeled by the next wave. Then, someday after my generation is forgotten, it will be noted that the tide was turned against mindless waste, that solar, wind and ocean power sources have become staples of life on earth. I hope that scenario will prevail, and if it does, I believe we should recognize that the credit should go to people like Jim DeKorne, who says in this book: "If you want to change the world, change your own life."

J-Y C
November 1976

Preface

The sun is the primal force of life, and from it all life springs. It tempers earth, wind, water, and light. It makes plants, crops, and trees grow. The sun's energy literally determines the survival of the human race. Yet in our dependence on diminishing fossil fuels we turn our backs to the one dependable source for our future. A classic discussion of this dilemma was raised by Farrington Daniels in his book *Direct Use of the Sun's Energy*, first published in 1964. (Now available in paperback through Ballantine Books.) Daniels pointed out that a quarter of the world's fossil fuel consumption goes into space heating. He also noted that there were at that time very few solar-heated buildings with a heat storage system in the world. Could this gap be narrowed, if not bridged? A handful of people cared enough to try. While others were assaulting the moon and wasting billions of dollars in colonial wars, only about two hundred solar houses were built between 1964 and 1976 (at a cost infinitely lower than the price of one supersonic bomber!). What is more important than the actual number of solar buildings on record is the fact that those pioneering with solar housing have established the feasibility of tapping a limitless energy source. They have shown how available technology could develop an inexhaustible and nonpolluting alternative to fossil fuels. It has proven to be an alternative with a positive energy gain (unlike nuclear reaction or coal gasification). It can be controlled at an individual and community level. And it is *free*.

Who are the people who designed and built the first solar houses? What is it like to live intimately (and freely) with sun, earth, and wind? What does their experience mean to us today and tomorrow? To find the answers we took a sounding of the solar pioneers, the sun and wind developers and their supporter-clients, the backyard do-it-yourselfers, the tinkerers, the homesteaders, and the social changers—who are the cutting edge of the solar- and natural-energy community. The result is a book of reportage done primarily in the states of New Mexico, Colorado, California, Oregon, Washington, Minnesota, Tennessee, New York, New Jersey, Connecticut, Rhode Island, and Maine. We touched base where the bulk of solar activity is going on. Certainly important work in the field is being done elsewhere, and on another trip we hope to visit some of the people we missed. By concentrating our focus, we gained sharp insight into the tremendous vitality and involvement of people in different regions, at different seasons. In the Southwest and Midwest it was winter, in the Northwest it was spring, and in California almost summer; the East was a mixture of winter, spring, and summer. This gave us a simultaneous reading on the effects of solar heating in a variety of microclimates. What we found was positive both in the expression of its forms and in its commitment to a life in accord with nature.

Connecting the world of those who live with sun, wind, and earth, we found, is a spirit of optimism, a faith that something can be done about the environment and a pride in what has been done. To the extent that we shared this spirit with those who gave so generously to this book, we are most grateful. To the extent that we can pass on their spirit and their experience to others, we shall be most satisfied.

Acknowledgments

First and foremost, I must thank the readers of the Sunday *Magazine* of *The New York Times* who were the first to alert me to the public's insatiable curiosity about solar energy by their tremendous response to two articles, published in 1974 and 1975. Their letters and phone calls for more information about the houses, about the people who lived in them, about the whole question of conservation and alternate sources of energy in general, gave me both the book's idea and its title, *Design for a Limited Planet.*

Next, I must thank my co-author, Jon Naar, who, from my casual mention of a book over what became an especially eventful lunch, offered to photograph these fascinating living environments. (Many of them were so new when he arrived on their doorsteps that the paint was wet on the walls and the solar collectors were humming for their very first season.) His trip across the country to photograph the families and to be my eyes and ears in absentia, was of necessity a difficult one. It's hard to balance a camera in one hand and a pad and pencil in the other.

Thus, I must thank all of the owners of the houses who gave so generously of their time to my seemingly endless phone calls to amplify the rough notes, to clarify a thought, to untangle a quote, and to expand on the hard facts and figures of cost and cost savings. Especially helpful were Kent Bloomer, Richard Davis, William Smith III, Daniel Newman, Mrs. Douglas Boleyn, Richard Smith, Dennis Holloway, and Neil Welliver. Harold Hay deserves a special mention for his unqualified cooperation and patience during my two hour-long phone calls to California, and Richard Crowther, for calls almost as long to Denver. Don Frey, his tireless associate, worked with me at outrageous hours, the worst being over a July 4th weekend, and helped me out by offering technical data from the firm's own book *Sun/Earth: How to Use Solar and Climatic Energies Today.* The crew at 519 East Eleventh Street were nothing short of fantastic, not only for their courageous resuscitation of a whole city block, but also for the hours of interviews that the co-op members granted me, especially the unofficial Mayor of the Lower East Side, Roberto Nazario; the house intellectual, Michael Freedberg; the lady shop steward of the carpenter's local there, Karen Berman; and, last but not least, the house's dashing bachelor, Joe B. Barnes. With a crew like that it's obvious that New York City is alive and well!

A very special thanks must go to Esteban Habiague, whose fine curiosity about energy alternatives gave me the outsider's point of view. A wizard at untangling volts, watts, and amperage, it was he who came up with an analogy on how electricity works that any layman could understand.

No one really knows the blood, sweat, and tears that the book went through more than my courageous editor at Ballantine Books, Julie Colmore. Her ability to strengthen a weak sentence and pull out just the right adjective or adverb was truly miraculous. To her, my profound thanks.

Norma Skurka
November 1976

I wish to thank above all Travis Price for his most important contributions to the book. First, in its developmental stages, he freely gave ideas, material, and personal leads, inspiring both the photography and the interviewing that I did in the field. In a second capacity, as my technical consultant, he reviewed all the material for technical accuracy. Wearing a third hat—a Stetson, naturally—his image appears in many parts of the book as builder, consultant, designer, architect, and solar mover extraordinary: in the Eddy House in Rhode Island and at 519 East Eleventh Street, New York City, the first urban tenement building to use solar energy; he was also involved as a member of the Sun Mountain Design group in the designing and building of the Wright, Nichols, Allers, and other solar projects in New Mexico. In a real sense Travis Price guided my travels to the sun and my safe return to earth. It was quite a trip! Without his help and encouragement my part in the book would have been well nigh impossible. I am most grateful to him and to Ron Eichorn of Guilford, Connecticut, who introduced Price to me at the outset.

Through Price I was most fortunate to meet in Santa Fe the incomparable Bill Lumpkins on the first day of my journey through most of solar U.S.A. The combination of Price's introductions and Lumpkins's generosity opened virtually every door for me in New Mexico. This included Keith Haggard and Susan Yanda of the New Mexico Solar Energy Association, Peter van Dresser, Bill Yanda, Wayne and Susan Nichols, David and Barbara Wright, and many others who, it seemed to me, stopped everything else they were doing to help me on this project. Price had put me in touch with an ever expanding network of solar friendship and love. I was passed on literally from the Wrights to Karen Terry, through whom I met Georgine McGowan, who showed me the path to Taos and beyond. Carolyn Allers took me to El Rito, New Mexico, where we spent an unforgettably beautiful day with Jim and Elizabeth DeKorne and their survival homestead. From DeKorne to Bill Yanda and eventually to the omniscient Lee Johnson, editor of *Rain* magazine, in Portland, Oregon. Lee sent me to Ken Smith and other friends at Ecotope in the state of Washington, and from there to Farallones Institute in Berkeley and Occidental, California. In Colorado I was generously received by Dr. George Löf, Richard Pence, Carl Lehrburger, and Richard Crowther.

I would also like to record my warm gratitude to Lee Porter Butler in San Francisco for the many kindnesses and insights he gave me; to Howdy Reichmuth, who gave me the dedication for this book and much more; to Dennis Holloway at Ouroboros in Minneapolis and St. Paul; to Everett Barber in Guilford, Connecticut; to Louise and Junius Eddy in Little Compton, Rhode Island; to Neil Welliver in Maine; to David Sellers in Vermont; to my twelve-year-old son, Alexander, who with Mark Bloomer put this energy problem in the right perspective (see page138). And finally, my special thanks to Mark's father. Kent Bloomer, who got me started on the whole cosmic journey in the first place!

It is my hope that the excitement and the spirit of the people mentioned above and others I got to know and who shared so much of themselves with me in doing this book will be reflected in the pages that follow.

Jon Naar
November 1976

Key to Symbols used in Diagrams

The diagrams shown in this book to illustrate how solar heating systems work, all use the following symbols:

Masonry

Concrete

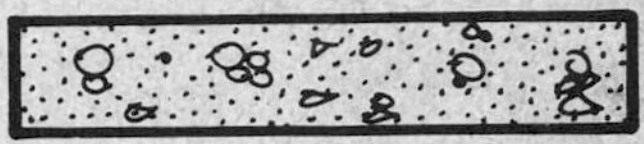

Stucco or plaster

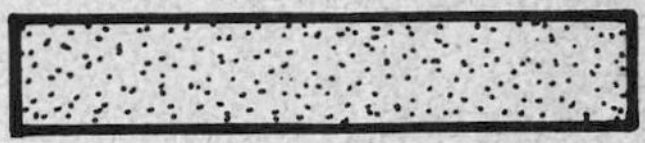

Earth or gravel fill

Soil or grade level

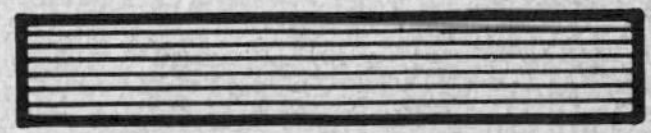

Rigid insulation, such as styrofoam or polyurethane panels

Fiberglass batt insulation

Air flow

Cool air

Angle of the sun's radiation

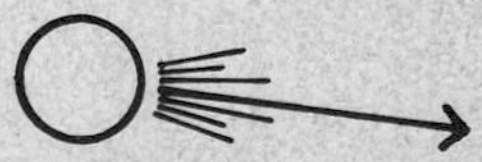

Heat radiation

Fan

Introduction
Nothing New under the Sun

Solar radiation is mankind's greatest energy resource. The amount of energy that the earth receives from the sun each day is colossal. It is roughly 100,000 times more than the present world output of power from all the operating utility plants. Two days of solar radiation falling on the surface of the earth equals the world's total fossil fuel reserves.

Clean, free, and plentiful—few alternative energy sources present as enticing a picture as the sun and wind. Sunbeams and breezes fall everywhere and on everybody, more or less evenly around the world. Solar and wind power are conveniently distributed and need no power grid. As nations vie for the remaining stores of fossil fuel, the so-called natural energy sources, sun and wind, assume an enormous appeal.

Solar energy is the quintessential clean energy. Whereas fossil fuels pose serious pollution problems, sunshine is safe and efficient. Coal is dangerous to mine, dirty to burn, and a major air pollutant. Gas is cheap but only because the government regulates its price. In any case, it is threatened with near-term depletion. At the present rate of consumption, the United States may burn its last molecule of natural gas within the next twenty years. Nuclear power, hailed as recently as two decades ago with messianic fervor, has become a serious menace and a potentially lethal source of power. Waste products from nuclear power plants create a deadly pollution threat to the world. A news article in *The New York Times* stated that the radiation level of the Atlantic shoreline was rising as a result of leakage from nuclear waste containers dumped in the ocean. The containers were deposited there within the past ten years—what can happen during the course of the *next* 250,000 years when these wastes continue to remain lethal? In addition, plutonium, an essential ingredient of the atomic bomb, and a by-product of nuclear fission, is vulnerable to theft. There already may be enough missing to foster an international nuclear black market.

The spiraling cost of fuel, which we all see reflected in our monthly utility bills, brings the fossil fuel shortage into our own backyards. Projections indicate that the prices of oil and natural gas are likely to rise even more steeply in the near future. Some studies say that gas prices will rise 300 percent by 1990 and that electricity will cost 125 percent more. Electricity is already the most costly of energy sources (except in the vicinity of a hydroelectric plant). Nobody who has looked at the past performance can believe that the proposed nuclear power plants will lower the cost of electricity. In truth, nuclear power plants are producing electricity at a much higher cost than was envisioned in the 1950s and 1960s. This, coupled with the dangerous waste and pollution threat, has eroded even the government's interest in nuclear power. With such a grim prelude, the sun and wind loom as the least exploited, least hazardous, most ecologically benign of all energy alternatives.

Ironically, the inordinate dependence on fossil fuel is a recent development. Since the advent of cheap, imported oil from the 1960s onward, America has consumed more energy than many an underdeveloped nation has used in its entire history. This energy joyride has made the United States the world's biggest energy consumer. With 6 percent of the world's population, this country consumes one-third of the world's energy, according to an article on solar energy in *Progressive Architecture*, May 1975.

On the home front, the ethic of energy conservation and environmental restraint has been neglected in most architecture of the past forty years. We have been creating buildings so out of tune with nature that the windows cannot be opened in summer and lights burn twenty-four hours a day, especially true of commercial and institutional high-rise buildings. House design ignores all aspects of siting and beneficial topography that could work in concert with nature to warm and cool the structure. A house is primarily a place of shelter from the extremes of weather—heat, cold, rain, wind, and snow. But in modern times, the house has become a vault where a flick of a switch changes, regulates, or creates its own interior climate. We depend upon modern gadgetry, run at a tremendous cost of energy, to assault, affront, and challenge nature, when, with intelligent design rather than mechanical muscle, nature could perform most of the functions of the heating and cooling.

We will certainly have to change our ways to reverse this trend. The energy used in the home accounts for about 33 percent of the nation's total energy consumption. In Sweden, where the standard of living is slightly higher than it is here, the average consumer uses *one-half* the amount of energy required by his American counterpart.

Heating of the house takes the largest chunk out of the total domestic energy use, and air conditioning takes the next largest amount. Fuel for the house's hot water supply accounts for another hefty slice. If solar energy could perform at least two of these three functions, and many scientists believe that it can, we would cut down sharply on the enormous energy drain that the home represents. Some scientists predict that within five years, solar-powered systems for heating and cooling homes will be commercially available at prices competitive with gas or oil furnaces and electric air conditioners.

But this is not a book of dry statistics; it is about people getting back in touch with nature. It is a book about reestablishing the intangible links that exist between man and his environment, links that give self-sufficiency and satisfaction to human existence. Throughout the book, we sense the tremendous joy that the solar pioneers gain from becoming on intimate terms with the elements. The quotes, which come from every householder who lives in a solar house, celebrate this newfound adventure.

Changing lifestyles have dominated the headlines for the past five years or so. We hear about people who aim for greater self-reliance: to make things with their hands, to grow their own food, to garden, to take an active stand against the intrusion into their lives by the government, utility companies, and big business. It is a new wave of grass-roots return-to-the-land philosophy that engenders an almost spiritual renewal for those who try it.

Solar energy and wind power are reviving the pioneer spirit that settled America. But that sense of rediscovery is best left to the words of those who experienced it. Our task is merely to open up the field of new ideas and to provide the starting point to others who may want to explore the potential of natural energy.

There are pitfalls in trying out a new lifestyle and a new way of living, as there are in any fledgling endeavor. By reading and sharing the experiences of others, we hope that we can alert you to the trouble areas and help you to avoid the worst. Natural energy demands a whole new sense of design, and it will drastically alter the look and livability of the house. Designing for natural energy starts with the very ground on which the house sits and the trees that surround it—and continues all the way up to the roof peak and sky.

History

There is literally nothing new under the sun. The newly popular "natural" energy sources, the sun and wind, have been used by mankind since antiquity. Harnessing these power sources is not even new technology. The sun's rays have heated homes and domestic water, either directly or indirectly, for centuries. Residential markets for solar- and wind-energy devices flourished in America in recent memory. Between the turn of the·century and the 1930s, solar water heaters were used extensively in California and Florida. Tens of thousands of these glass-faced, black-painted metal boxes were set out on the rooftops to furnish a house's hot water supply. More than 5,000 homes in the Southwest and Florida still use solar water heaters today. They are also used in Israel, North Africa, Japan, and in Australia, where solar water heating is mandatory. In Japan alone, 160,000 water heaters were sold in 1974 and more than 2½ million are in operation—heating one-quarter of all the baths taken by the Japanese today.

Quixotic as the wind can be, it has been pumping water, milling grain, and sailing ships from ancient times. Some historians believe that wind machines were developed as early as 2000 B.C. in the Near East. Early settlers in America made use of windmills from the seventeenth century onward, some of which are still standing as historic monuments on Long Island, in New York and in New Jersey. Prior to the Rural Electrification Act in the 1930s, wind generators supplied the electricity to farms across the U.S. These machines, powered exclusively by the wind, could deliver between 400 and 500 kilowatt-hours of electricity per month, or enough to supply the essential needs for a farm family. Between 1928 and 1957, the Jacobs Wind Electric Company of Minneapolis, Minnesota, sold $75 million worth of their wind machines. These wind generators can still be found straddling old towers in remote farm regions. Prized for their efficiency and reli-

Windmills, such as this historic landmark near Newport, Rhode Island (right), were a familiar sight on the Colonial American landscape.

ability, they are easily reclaimed when found in good condition. Jacobs machines, old as they are, find a ready market among today's generation of wind enthusiasts. (The name crops up time and again in the chapters on wind power in this book.)

Western science has been exploring the possibilities of the direct use of the sun for energy since the seventeenth century, when the German inventor Athanasius Kircher used fine mirrors to focus the sun's rays enough to ignite a woodpile. The eighteenth century saw numerous experiments for powering steam engines and heating ovens by solar radiation. In the nineteenth century, a solar steam engine ran the printing press for the newspaper *Le Soleil* in Paris. Research into ways to make use of the sun has continued sporadically since then. There have been successful experiments in desalinating water, cooking food, and firing solar ovens. These ovens, developed for commercial use, could reach temperatures of several thousands of degrees Fahrenheit by means of special devices that focus the sun's rays. Devices to collect or capture the sun's radiation are called solar collectors. The high-powered collectors are called "focusing" collectors because they make use of special lenses that concentrate the sunlight, or "parabolic" collectors, dish-shaped devices with mirrored or polished surfaces that also intensify and focus the sun's rays. While the high temperatures generated by focusing and parabolic collectors are necessary for industrial uses, they are impractical for home use.

In 1908 a collector that was almost ideal for domestic use was developed by Frank Shuman, an American scientist-inventor, who refined an even earlier design. Shuman built a small metal box that became the prototype for the so-called "flat plate" collector commonly in use today. Most of the houses with solar equipment shown in this book are equipped with a refined version of Shuman's basic unit. It consists of a metal box with the inside painted black and a transparent glass (or plastic) lid. If the box is faced into the sun, it is possible to heat the air inside the box to temperatures as high as 140 degrees Fahrenheit.

Shuman's invention was designed to power a steam engine rather than to heat a house. In fact, at that time, space heating was a minor consideration in solar-energy research. Between the years 1920 and 1950, little research activity occurred in the field, but since the 1950s, interest has grown steadily with symposia at Massachusetts Institute of Technology (M.I.T.), the University of Wisconsin, and the United Nations Conference on New Sources of Energy, held in Rome in 1961. Today, the small-scale use of solar energy-saving technology in individual homes is high priority for both researchers and industry.

From the late nineteen thirties through the

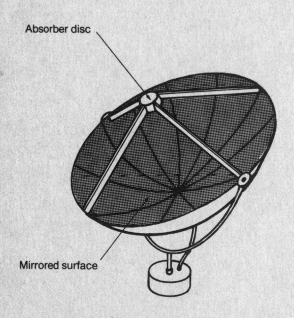

Absorber disc

Mirrored surface

Parabolic collector

early fifties, solar pioneers in the United States conducted experiments using special solar hardware—primarily flat plate solar collectors—to heat homes. At M.I.T., H.C. Hottel directed experiments with four buildings equipped with roof-mounted flat plate solar collectors. Other pioneers working in this area were Maria Telkes (who designed a solar-heated house in Dover, Massachusetts, in the middle 1940s), R. W. Bliss, G. O. G. Löf, and Peter van Dresser. (Löf's own house and one converted for solar energy in the 1950s by van Dresser are included in this book, pages 32 and 38.)

All of the experimenters mentioned utilized special equipment, such as solar collectors and other special hardware, to gain heat from the sun. There are and there have always been other ways to capture that heat. Two other solar pioneers have investigated simpler ways to harness the sun's heat. With John I. Yellott, Harold Hay worked out a system using ponds of water encased in plastic, like giant water beds, on the house roof (see Hay's Atascadero house, page 28). Felix Trombe, a French architect working in the Pyrenees who was primarily a builder of solar furnaces, experimented with massive thermal surfaces for space heating. He devised a heavy exterior masonry wall (now known as the Trombe wall), that faces south and is faced in glass with an air cavity in between. The otherwise sealed airspace between the glass and the masonry wall vents at the top and bottom to the interior of the building. Sun striking the glass heats the air in the cavity, which rises and exits through the top vent. In turn, cool air enters the vent near the floor level and is drawn into the cavity by natural convection where it is heated. At night, the sun-warmed masonry wall radiates its heat to the interior of the building. (A recently built house using this system is that of Douglas Kelbaugh shown on page 122.)

Since the oil embargo of October 1973, the interest in solar energy has intensified. Before 1960 there were fewer than ten solar houses in existence; a decade later there were thirty, and today, there are several hundred either completed or under construction. The prospects for the fledgling industry of solar energy for space and water heating are bright indeed. Arthur D. Little, a Cambridge, Massachusetts, market research firm, predicts that it will become a $1.3-billion industry by 1985.

At present, eleven states offer tax credits to homeowners who install solar heating systems. Those states are Arizona, California, Colorado, Illinois, Maryland, New Hampshire, New Mexico, North Dakota, Oregon, South Dakota and Texas. The remaining states are considering similar legislation.

The Federal government also has a bill pending that would give an income tax credit to homeowners for solar heating. The tax bill, already passed by the Senate and awaiting approval by the House of Representatives as of October 1976, would provide homeowners with a credit of up to $2000 for installing such a system. The $2000 credit would apply specifically to the cost of installing solar or geothermal heat collecting equipment for space heating. There are also other provisos in the bill for installing energy conserving materials. Homeowners, for instance, would be allowed to subtract from their taxes 30 percent of the first $750 they spend on insulation and weatherproofing, up to a maximum of $225. They would also receive a credit of up to $1000 for replacing electric baseboard-type heating with a heat pump.

If this bill becomes law, the tax credits would make solar heating systems competitive with conventional space heating systems. Not only that, the fuel savings and the resale value added to the house as a result of solar heating makes it much more attractive as an investment to homeowners.

The current questions on peoples' minds are: How does solar water and space heating actually function—and does it really work? Compared with the conventional methods for space and hot water heating, how efficient is it and how expensive is it? We will attempt to address these questions in the following pages.

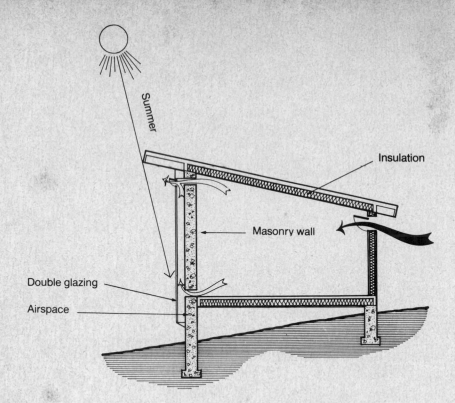

Summer

Insulation

Masonry wall

Double glazing

Airspace

Trombe wall – summer

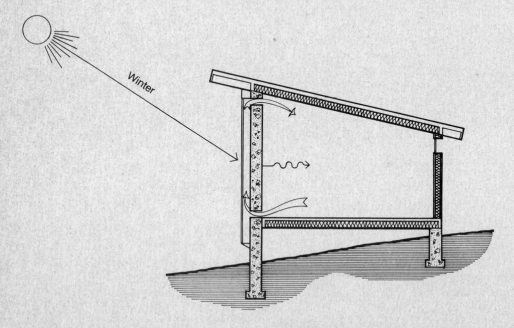

Winter

Trombe wall – winter

How Solar Heating Systems Work

Solar-systems can perform three basic functions for the house: they can heat the hot water supply, which is a relatively simple task; they can heat the interior spaces of the house, which is somewhat more difficult; and they can cool the house, which is the most complex of the three tasks. With all three functions, it is necessary to have a form of solar collector, a means to collect heat from the sun. Because the sunrays reach us only during the day, a solar heating system also requires some type of reservoir to store and retain the sun's heat and from which it can be retrieved as it is needed.

The basic principle behind a solar collector is not at all complex. Direct sunlight is a powerful space heater, as anyone knows who has left a car parked in the sun with the windows closed. The temperature inside the car builds up until it is almost intolerable. The same thing occurs within a greenhouse, where the sun's radiation enters the enclosed space through the glass walls. Upon hitting the surfaces, the sun's rays become infrared radiation—or heat. While glass is transparent to sunlight, it traps the infrared radiation, so the interior of the greenhouse becomes a collector for the heat. A greenhouse can generate large accumulations of air warmed by the sun to temperatures of 100 degrees Fahrenheit and above.

Most solar collectors work on a principle similar to the greenhouse effect. The units used to heat a house or its hot water supply are little more than groupings of a basic metal-backed box with a transparent lid (or several lids) of either glass or plastic. The metal of the back plate is painted black, because that is the most heat absorbent of all colors. The outside of the box is carefully sealed and insulated to avoid heat leaking through the back and sides. The box is angled to face into the sun. Air inside the box is heated by the sun to about 140 degrees.

Another version of the solar collector has pipes, usually of copper because of its superior heat conduction, that are affixed to the metal plate of the box. Water is circulated through the pipes to be heated by the sun. Both these versions of the solar collector are called "flat plate" collectors. The one

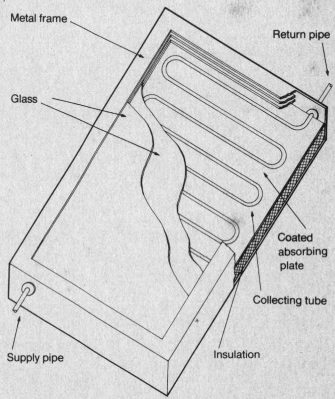

Water—type Flat Plate Collector

that works with air as the heat vehicle is a flat plate air-type collector, and the one in which water is the heat medium is a flat plate water-type collector.

The sun-heated air or water from the collector is piped down to a reservoir, where the heat can be "stored," and released at a later time, usually when the sun goes down and the house begins to get cold.

The key to the effectiveness of a solar heating system is the method used to store accumulated solar energy. The most common method is to store heat in a large body of material with good heat-retaining properties, such as rock, concrete, or water. In order for the storage medium to be able to retain the heat for long periods, it must also be particularly well insulated against leakage. Water is an advantageous storage medium, because not only is it cheap enough so that a very large storage capacity is possible, but it can serve both as the storage element and the vehicle—that is, it can be pumped from place to place.

There are two basic types of solar heating storage systems in use today: the "air-to-rock" system and the water collector system. As the name implies, the air-to-rock system utilizes a flat plate collector that circulates air as the heat vehicle. The hot air from the collectors circulates down to a bin of rocks or crushed stone, usually placed beneath the main living area of the house. In some systems, the floor directly over the rock bin is purposely left less insulated than the other sides of the bin to leak heat to the living space above, turning the floor into a radiant heat surface.

The solar water collector system utilizes flat plate collectors with pipes or troughs through which water circulates. The sun-heated water is piped from the collector into a water-filled storage tank, where it intermixes and, in effect, transfers its solar heat to the water in the tank. There is also a refined version of the solar water collector, called a "closed-loop" system, in which the water circulating between the solar collector and the water in the storage tank do not mix. Heat is exchanged by a series of metal coils that are laid closely together so that the heat is transferred through contact. Closed-loop systems are used primarily in cold northern climates where there is a chance of water in the collectors freezing after sundown. The closed-loop system also makes it possible to use a blend of water and ethylene glycol, better known as antifreeze, in the collector to guard against freezing that could damage the system.

Today, slightly less than half of the operating solar houses use air as the heat collection system. The advantage of air as a medium is that it eliminates the risk of damage from freezing in winter. The hot air transfers its heat from the collector to a bin of rock or crushed stone. The disadvantage of air as the storage vehicle (as opposed to water) is that air retains and conducts less heat. A given volume of stone and air will hold about 40 percent as much heat as an equal amount of stone and water, and only 20 percent as much heat as a like-sized tank of water.

Solar collectors are usually positioned on the side of the house facing south (or north in the southern hemisphere). They may be tilted at any angle between vertical and horizontal. For the greatest efficiency, the collector ideally should be angled nearly perpendicular to the sun's rays. But since the sun is a moving object, the collector would have to be able to track its movement in order to face the sun perpetually at the most efficient angle. Furthermore, the angle of the sun is generally lower at high latitudes than it is in more southern climes, and it is also lower in the morning and evening than at midday. Therefore, the angle at which sunlight strikes the earth's surface varies greatly according to geography and season. For this reason, solar experts have arrived at a general formula that collectors should be placed at the angle of the latitude plus about 15 to 20 degrees from the horizontal. This means that in low latitudes, the collectors will be nearly flat, while in higher latitudes they will be angled at a steeper pitch. In some regions, the collectors have been incorporated directly into the side walls of a building rather than mounted on the roof, which is the more common practice. To compensate for the loss of efficiency of the stationary collector, many solar engineers simply resort to installing additional footage of collectors on the house.

The ideal climate for a solar heating system is one with cold winters and plenty of sunshine. Such conditions occur, especially at high altitudes, but they are more the exception than the rule of weather patterns across the nation. The pattern and sequence of alternating sunny and cloudy conditions obviously affects how well the solar system will perform. The duration and frequency of cloudy periods in a location dictates the volume of thermal storage capacity required by a solar-heated house to carry it through a sunless period. Wind velocity in a region can seriously affect the performance of a solar collector. High winds increase the amount of heat lost to the sky from the face and body of the collector itself and can greatly reduce its performance.

The solar collector system for heating a building's water supply is simpler than the apparatus needed to heat the house. The most popular type is a flat plate water collector that preheats the hot water tank to about 100 to 120 degrees. This solar-heated water is then fed into a conventional gas- or electric-fired water heater for heating up to the required 130 or 140 degrees. This initial boost can cut down on fuel consumption to a considerable degree, in many areas, as much as 90 percent of the hot water supply bill.

Another system for heating hot water is the thermosiphon water collector, which circulates the water by gravity. Hot water rises naturally because it is less dense than cold water. As a result, with this system the solar collectors have to be positioned lower than the water storage tank, generally about 2 feet below it. When the water in the storage tank is cooler than that in the solar collector, water flows down into the collector to be heated. As it is heated, the warm water rises and returns to the storage tank by natural convection.

The size of a solar collector needed to heat a house and its hot water adequately is dependent on a host of factors. It is necessary to assess the climate and to analyze how long the system will have to weather a period of sunless days, when the house will be dependent on heat remaining in the storage tank. The size of the house, its heating requirements, and how well it is insulated are additional considerations. The roughest rule of thumb devised by solar engineers is that the surface area of the solar collector should be equal to about one-half the total floor space of the house. But this is by no means a hard-and-fast formula. A location in a high-wind area or a particularly misty and cloudy one can greatly reduce a solar system's efficiency.

At the present time, few houses can rely totally upon a solar heating system for all space and water heating needs. In some states, if a house is to pass the local building codes, an auxiliary heat source is mandatory. This can be anything from a wood-burning furnace, fireplace, or Franklin stove, to a conventional oil- or gas-fired furnace or electric baseboard heating. However, in most houses that are solar heated, their owners claim that the solar system supplies somewhere between 50 to 90 percent of their heating needs.

There are essentially two ways to cool a house by solar energy. One uses the sun in a passive, or nonmechanical way, and the other utilizes the same solar hardware that heats the house.

Solar, or natural cooling, like passive solar heating, results first from sound building logic. The same energy-conserving principles and changes in design, materials and building methods used to heat the house in winter work to keep the house cool in summer. If the building is well insulated, for instance, it resists the build-up of excessive heat from the summer sun just as it resists heat loss during the winter. Deciduous trees which shield the house from the summer sun are also highly effective in keeping the house interiors cool.

Judicious placement of the windows to allow for a natural air flow through the building is another important way to cool down the interiors. Many of the houses shown in this book have small air intake vents, located close to ground level on the north side of the house to allow an inflow of cool night air. Other vents, located higher up, beneath the roof eaves on the south side, create a suction that draws in the cool air as it expels the hot air from the roof vents. This suction, or chimney effect, follows the natural law that hot air rises while cooler air falls. At the height of summer, fans located at the top of the house help to create the necessary air flow through the house.

The Harold Hay house in Atascadero, California (page 28), is a unique example of another natural solar cooling system. The medium that heats the house—huge, water-filled plastic bags laid across the house roof—is the same medium that effectively cools it. For example, in winter the water ponds, exposed to the sun all day, absorb the heat. At night, large, insulated roof panels are closed over the water ponds. The heat from the ponds radiates down into the house interior through a metal ceiling. The process reverses itself for summer cooling. During the day, the insulated roof panels are kept closed to hold down the heat build-up in the interior of the house. The thermal ponds, however, are absorbing the excess heat build-up through the metal ceilings. At night, the roof panels are opened and this heat is then released to the cooler night air.

Harold Hay admits that the main drawback to this cooling system is that it doesn't work in areas of high humidity, such as the Gulf Coast of Florida. There the night air is too full of moisture to set up the evaporation of heat needed to cool down the water ponds on top of the house.

Except for these two methods of solar cooling or, more accurately, natural cooling, most of the other cooling systems have to utilize mechanical hardware. The most common device used with the solar heating system is the heat pump. During the summer, the heat pump acts very much like an air conditioner. When we walk past an air conditioner from the outside, we are hit by a blast of hot air. Inside the house, as we know, the air conditioner is letting off a blast of cool air. The heat pump works like a reversible air conditioner. It is able to produce either warm or cool air and can circulate this warm or cool air through the house depending upon the season.

For the purposes of creating heat, the heat pump which is electrically operated, is far cheaper than running an electric baseboard heater. This is not the case for its cooling operation, however. Using the heat pump to cool air, in place of a true air conditioner, the cost savings would be negligible.

That is why solar cooling is still considered relatively rudimentary and why a great deal of experimentation is still going on. Except for the passive ways to cool the building interiors, solar cooling has a long way to go to represent enough of a cost saving to make it worthwhile.

One of the few drawbacks of installing a solar heating system is the complicated logistics of assembling the working parts. It is not yet possible although it may be soon) to purchase a complete system "off the shelf" at one source as it is with conventional heating systems. Anyone who is interested in solar heating has to contact several outlets, starting with a source for the collectors, and yet another for the pipes, pumps, and plumbing. The next step is to locate or build an appropriate storage reservoir (be it a rock bin or water tank) and tie the whole system together. It is a complicated and intricate process and one that is rapidly becoming more sophisticated. A prospective solar-home owner would be well advised to consult with the experts, either someone who has built and lived in a solar-heated house or an architect or engineer who specializes in such systems. Most of the pioneers who have undertaken to live in solar houses have done so out of deep moral conviction. They are joyously open about their experiences and more than willing to share them with kindred spirits.

Designing for Solar Energy

If the house is to be less wasteful of energy, its basic design must change radically. Anyone who imagines that converting a house for solar heating means simply putting a row of solar collectors on the roof is badly misinformed. If a home owner acts on that premise, the investment in solar equipment will have been thrown away, because he will end up passing the winter months in an uncomfortably cool house. A solar heating system can only work efficiently in concert with other sound energy-conserving principles. The buildings that most of us inhabit are overheated in winter, overcooled in summer, and underinsulated—in short, they are inordinately wasteful of fuel. To turn the house around so that it saves rather than squanders fuel calls for a reexamination of the way it is designed and built, where it is sited, what it is built of, where the windows are placed, and how well it is insulated. This basic structure cannot be thought of as being isolated from solar technology. The two are inextricably linked if the solar system is to function properly. Solar energy demands a whole new sense of design.

We do not have to look far into the past to find habitations that functioned in harmony with nature rather than in opposition to it, as they do today. Up until recent times, house design was a response to the local climate and to indigenous materials. The shape of the building, such as the four-square New England farmhouse of a century ago, or the southern plantation house rimmed by verandas, gave architecture a regionalism. In humid climes houses were open and airy, with the living area raised on the second level to gain natural ventilation from prevailing breezes. Conversely, where cold and heavy snowfalls prevailed, houses were sheltered and enclosed with small windows and steeply pitched roofs. Nature dictated where the house was situated—some nestled into the side of a hill, others grouped together with outbuildings to provide wind protection. Early New England houses and those on the Great Plains traditionally had the windows on the southern exposure, leaving the walls mostly unbroken to the north, where the prevailing winds blew strongest.

Houses were built of locally abundant materials: fieldstone, masonry, adobe, or wood framing stuffed with an insulating mix of mud and straw. The thermal mass of these thick walls gave inherent heat-retaining properties to the building. The walls built up heat during the day and released it slowly at night. Shutters, roof overhangs, deep window recesses, awnings, and other shading devices helped to keep the house naturally cool in summer.

Landscaping played an important role. Evergreen trees were planted as windbreaks where needed. Deciduous trees were strategically placed so that when they lost their leaves in winter, the sun would penetrate and warm the house interiors and yet shade the building in summer.

However, with the advent of modern architecture in the 1930s, much of this commonsense thinking and practical building knowledge vanished. They were replaced by the concept of "functionalism" that ignored the climate, the site's topography, and natural windbreaks. Speculative builders arbitrarily placed their houses side by side, creating the monotonous streetscape of the development project and contributing to the homeowners' high fuel bills.

Simple changes in the design of the conventional house can effect impressive fuel savings—without spending a penny on solar hardware. They involve reestablishing the principles that early builders used in the construction of their houses, such as orienting a building to the sun's passage across the sky as well as to the prevailing wind patterns and natural windbreaks, or by making the north side of the house, which receives the worst wind buffeting, relatively and windowless, and by allowing the largest windows to face south, where the sun will heat the interiors. Backing a house against a hillside or banking it with earth on the north is an age-old insulating technique. The Pueblo Indians understood this principle in the twelfth century and set the multifamily adobe dwellings of their community at Chaco Canyon against a steep hillside.

The use of large plate glass windows and window walls in modern times is a mixed blessing. On the one hand, a large expanse of glass facing the south is often adequate to heat a house on sunny winter days, regardless of the outdoor temperature. Indeed, many houses that call themselves solar-heated are nothing more than a well-insulated structure with large, south-facing window walls and few or no windows on the other sides. The solar heat gain is so powerful that many owners of such houses claim that the buildings get too hot on sunny days, even with zero-degree weather outside. After sundown, however, those houses cool rapidly because those same windows are responsible for a huge heat drain, as interior heat is lost by conduction through the plate glass to the cold outside air. Double-insulating glass, or that which consists of two sheets with an air space in between (also known as double-glazing or Thermopane), cuts down dramatically on the heat loss through windows. Shutters, thick draperies, and other insulating devices placed over the windows in the evening also help to retard heat loss.

The sleek look of the modern house eliminated two other practical, energy-saving features: roof overhangs and vestibules. The principle behind the roof overhang is sound: in summer, when the sun is high in the sky, the overhang shields the window areas of the house and reduces the solar heat gain inside, while in winter, when the sun moves in a lower arc, it misses the overhang and shines directly into the house, thereby warming the interiors. Vestibules were a common feature in American houses of the North: They created an air lock between the cold outside air and the warm interior air. Without a vestibule, every time the door is opened to the cold outdoors, about half of the heat in the entrance room is lost. In the Dakotas, most turn-of-the-century houses had an L-shaped vestibule with the entry door facing south. Home owners used this sun-warmed space to dry wet clothes. Because they create an effective insulating pocket, vestibules are now finding their way back into house design.

In Colonial days, the house was always built around the central chimney. The smokestack

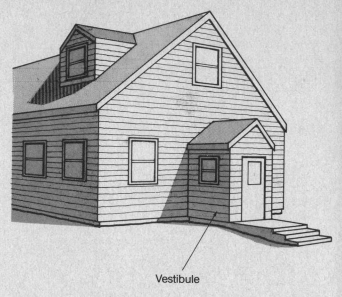

Vestibule

heated the surrounding rooms as much by radiation as by actual heat from the fire. Today, many chimneys are placed on the outside wall of the house. To conserve energy, they should be reinstated back to the center of the house.

Strangely, housing construction has not changed radically in the past hundred years. Following the Chicago fire of 1871, building techniques became standardized. Developed then and still an industry mainstay is the use of two-by-four-inch posts, or studs, on 16-inch centers to frame a house. Solar-energy advocates claim that this framing technique is clearly obsolete in face of the energy crisis. The two-by-four-inch studs leave a cavity between the inner and outer walls of less than 4 inches for insulation. Today, the recommended thickness of insulation for wood-framed buildings is closer to 6 or 7 inches in the exterior walls and up to 9 inches in the roof. Clearly, a larger stud has to be substituted, and the American Wood Council recommends the use of a two-by-six stud because it makes a cavity for insulation nearly 6 inches deep. Rather than spacing the two-by-six studs on 16-inch centers, the Council also advocates spacing them 24 inches apart. Insulation is now being manufactured in the new, wider, 24-inch widths to anticipate the change in construction standards, which can (and should) become widespread throughout the industry. Wood in itself is a good insulator, so wood framing in combination with the 6-inch-thick posts and 6 inches of insulation would create a much more substantial "skin" to the energy-conscious house.

Unfortunately, many of the building codes throughout the country prohibit such energy-saving construction changes. Most of these codes were formulated for a time when there were no energy shortages, and they now need to be completely reexamined and updated to meet the conditions of the times.

Because the conventional house is so wasteful of energy resources, it is difficult to convert the existing structure for solar-energy heating. First, it entails correcting all the mistakes built into the structure itself. Usually the house must be completely reinsulated, its windows weather-stripped and all cracks and air leaks sealed. Storm windows and double-insulating glass have to replace ordinary plate glass windows; basements, ceilings, and attics must be checked for heat loss. Indeed, in most instances, solar collectors cannot be added because the house itself is not properly placed on the site or because the angle of the roof is inadequate for such a conversion.

Whether we like it or not, the energy problem will have a profound effect on the look of houses and on the future of architecture. Superficial styling will most likely give way to realistic problem-solving. These are auspicious times for architectural design because there is now a strong base, a rationality, a form-generating purpose to design. Some of the directions that architecture will take—the experimental new forms and exploration into new and indigenous materials, the revival of practical building methods—are already evident in the houses shown in this book.

Harold Hay

Passive solar design, which uses little or no mechanical hardware, is the principle behind Harold Hay's ingeniously simple solar system. He tried out the concept on this one-story concrete block house in Atascadero, California. The designer stands outside, in front of the house that has come to be considered a landmark of solar architecture.

"Unless we make some radical changes every house we build today will continue to waste energy for the next forty years."

In many ways, Harold Hay is the mentor of the current generation of solar practitioners. The solar-heated house that Hay built in the hills of Atascadero, California, in September 1973, has the earmarks of genius about it. It is more economical than most other solar systems on the market, has fewer working parts than all but the most non-mechanical systems, and has built-in air conditioning. It uses only standard materials that are readily available. Hay built it as a demonstration house, the second in the United States. He first experimented with environmental building in India in the 1950s and in 1967 erected his first prototype solar house with J. I. Yellott, another solar pioneer, in Arizona.

Most solar-heated houses have complicated systems to gather the sun's heat. Nonmechanical, passive solar houses, even though they do not use collecting devices, are designed as heat traps that store the energy during the day to radiate back into the house at night. Harold Hay's house in Atascadero is conceived differently. It is designed for climate control of the interior, providing heat in winter and cooling in summer. The system is so simple that it has no moving parts except for insulating panels which open or close twice a day. The panels are controlled by a half-horsepower motor that runs a daily total of six minutes.

How does his system work? It consists of a flat-roofed house with water reservoirs, like large water beds, atop it. (Hay calls them "thermal ponds.") In winter, they absorb the sun's heat during the day. Beneath the ponds is a metal ceiling that radiates the stored heat into the interiors of the house. Insulated panels that slide across the tops of the ponds regulate the flow of heat, either into the house or out to the night sky. The process reverses for natural summer air conditioning, or "nocturnal cooling," whereby the heat built up in the house during the day, rises and is absorbed through the metal ceiling by the thermal ponds. At night, the insulated panels are opened and the heat is released into the night air.

Hay compares this heat transfer of the thermal ponds to that of asphalt pavement: "When black pavement gets so hot on a summer day that you can't walk barefoot on it, that's solar heating. The next morning, it's too cold to walk on barefoot and it wasn't air conditioning that cooled it but the heat going off to the night sky. That's what happens on my roof." Hay uses plastic bags to hold the water because plastic is a highly efficient heat dissipater (unlike glass) although not as efficient as a heat collector. It makes the system suitable for both heating and air conditioning.

Hay, an articulate, active, and dapper sexagenarian, describes himself as an inventor, although his formal training was in chemistry. His father was also an inventor, who came to the United States from Denmark and devised a pasteurizing process for dairy farmers. Hay has often switched fields, researching history, genetics, and dermatology, and was a visiting scholar at the Smithsonian Institution, but he always returns to solar research. He became absorbed with the problem of natural heating and cooling while in India as a United Nations building materials advisor to the Indian government. "We had to design buildings in which the population could live comfortably without electricity," he recalls. "The people had nothing but cow dung to heat their homes or even to cook with. I had to throw Western technology away and start back with nature and with what the people lived in traditionally—thick-walled dwellings that worked with the climate."

Hay's thoughts returned to insulation, his specialty. "Why not put insulation on wheels, tapping the outside climate for heat and cold, rolling the insulation to trap the heat in or to release it? That's what we do with clothing, after all," he said. This description of insulating panels that move like barn doors on aluminum tracks forms the basis for the regulation of heating and cooling of Hay's thermal pond house.

Unlike other systems, Hay's thermal ponds do not generate high temperatures; water in them averages around 85 degrees, so that they are not as efficient at supplying hot water. The water for the Atascadero house is preheated in the ponds to 100 degrees and then boosted by a conventional

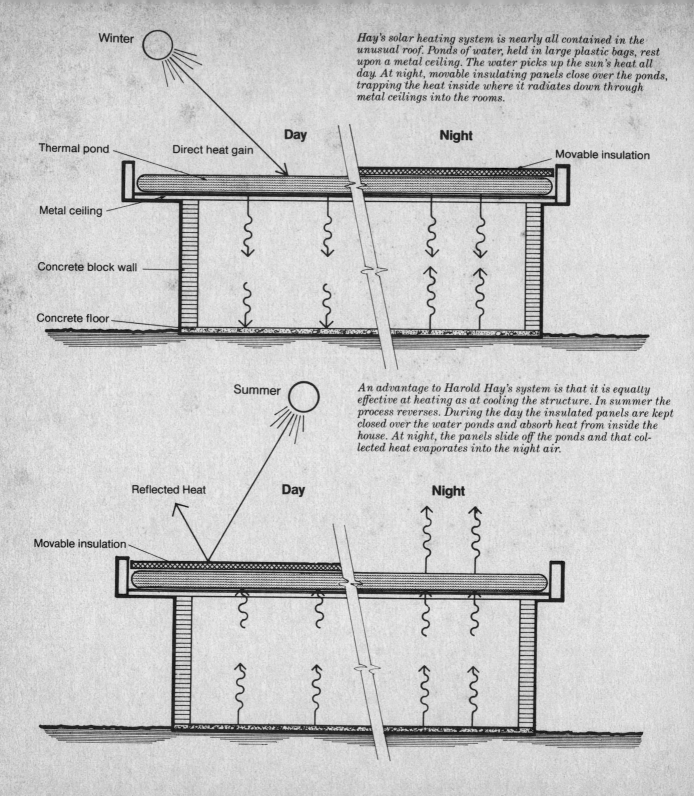

Hay's solar heating system is nearly all contained in the unusual roof. Ponds of water, held in large plastic bags, rest upon a metal ceiling. The water picks up the sun's heat all day. At night, movable insulating panels close over the ponds, trapping the heat inside where it radiates down through metal ceilings into the rooms.

Winter

Day

Night

Thermal pond

Direct heat gain

Movable insulation

Metal ceiling

Concrete block wall

Concrete floor

An advantage to Harold Hay's system is that it is equally effective at heating as at cooling the structure. In summer the process reverses. During the day the insulated panels are kept closed over the water ponds and absorb heat from inside the house. At night, the panels slide off the ponds and that collected heat evaporates into the night air.

Summer

Reflected Heat

Day

Night

Movable insulation

gas heater to 140 degrees.

The low, steady temperatures result in a very pleasant interior temperature that is uniform throughout the house, with no warm or cold spots. A family of five who moved into the house in September 1973 kept comfortable year-round without any auxiliary source for heat or cooling. The three-bedroom, two-bathroom house is built of concrete block to support the weight of the thermal ponds which hold roughly 6,000 gallons of water.

The house was monitored for performance by a research team from California Polytechnic State University at San Luis Obispo. They concluded that the house, which is marketed by Hay's firm, Skytherm Processes and Engineering, in Los Angeles, could be built for only $2 more per square foot than a conventional house, and that the additional expenses would be quickly offset by the savings in utility bills. Heating and cooling account for half of the average homeowner's utility bills, says the California Poly team, noting that the only expense incurred in operating Hay's system is the use of the small, thermostatically controlled electric motor to move the roof panels. "Or, you could cut out that electricity by returning to the method used on my first Arizona prototype, and pull a rope twice a day," Hay says.

The strong point of Hay's solar system has been its downfall in many ways. Government grants, such as those given by the Department of Housing and Urban Development, favor more expensive and complex systems. HUD pays the difference between the cost of a conventional house and a solar house. It hardly pays for the builder to go through the paperwork and red tape for the small extra amount of money that Hay's system adds to the overall cost of building a house. "So the government subsidizes the high-priced systems and makes it impossible for low-cost systems like mine to get adopted on a national scale," he reasons.

In northern climates, Hay modifies the system by placing the thermal ponds under a shed roof with the south side faced in double-insulated glass. The slope of the roof sheds the snowfall. Otherwise, the system operates much the way it does in a southerly climate. The nocturnal cooling, or natural air conditioning, is not effective in high-humidity areas because of the reduced natural evaporation.

The Atascadero house has been rented out to private tenants who claim that the house maintains a uniformly comfortable temperature, with no warm or cold spots, regardless of the weather outside.

Hay also believes that solar advocates can be the movement's worst enemies. "The utility company in San Diego is putting up a house with flat plate solar collectors that costs $17,000 more than a conventional house and demonstrating it as a solar-energy house. They are demonstrating a disaster for solar energy," he says. "The answer will come out that it's uneconomical, too expensive. This is what kills solar energy."

Dr. Henry Marvin, director of the Division of Solar Energy for the Energy Research and Development Administration (ERDA), keeps two letters on his desk. One is from Harold Hay saying that solar energy should be implemented immediately and unless we make some radical changes every conventional house we build today will continue to waste energy for the next forty years. The other is from George Löf saying that solar energy is not yet economically feasible and that widespread use of it should be held off until more research is completed. He holds on to both statements to retain an objectivity and a perspective on this increasingly controversial subject.

George Löf

"In the 1960s there were nine solar buildings in the world.... Today...there are about two hundred....Tomorrow, there could be thousands."

Dr. George Löf is a well-known figure in solar-energy circles throughout the world. In the 1940s, along with Dr. Maria Telkes and Professor H. C. Hottel at the Massachusetts Institute of Technology, he did some of the earliest pioneering on the direct use of solar energy in the U.S. His work includes studies concerning cylindrical solar collectors, water desalination and solar dehumidification, solar-heated swimming pools, and solar stoves (he developed a portable, compact cooker that could boil a quart of water or grill a hot dog in twenty minutes).

In 1961, Löf wrote a classic review of solar house heating for the United Nations Conference on New Sources of Energy held in Rome. "At that time," Löf says, "there were nine solar buildings in the world, including my own house. Most were laboratories, rather than homes. Ten years later there were fewer than thirty solar houses. But today, the situation has changed dramatically because of the fuel crisis. Now there are about two hundred houses heated directly by the sun's energy, with another two or three hundred under contract. Tomorrow, there could be thousands."

Considering its pioneer status, the Löf house in suburban Denver, Colorado, is quite unobtrusive. It is remarkable for the fact that it has been in continuous operation since 1957 with virtually no alterations or major repairs. By an amusing coincidence, the day the house was photographed for this book, Löf was carrying out the first maintenance on the solar heating system since it was installed—replacing a few broken panes of glass on the roof collectors and adjusting the control mechanism in the house.

The system, which supplies 23 percent of the space heating today, is a straightforward air-to-rock system with flat plate collectors made of overlapping glass plates which are installed on the roof and angled to face south at 45 degrees. Air

Dr. George Löf, president of the 55-member nation International Solar Energy Society, holds a pane of ordinary plate glass that he used to surface the solar collectors on his house.

From either the front or back of the house (top and right), the solar collectors on the roof are hardly visible. The one-story ranch-style building blends in unobtrusively with that of its neighbors. There is a small patio on the front (top) and a solar heated swimming pool at the back (right). Above, Dr. Löf displays a chart, showing control data on the operation of his pioneering solar house.

passes behind the glass plates, where it is warmed by the sun, and passes through ducts to two 3-foot-wide, 18-foot-high cylinders inside the house that are filled with 12 tons of rocks. The hot air warms the rocks , which store the heat, to an average temperature of 140 degrees. The warm air is distributed through ducts to rooms in the house by a 1-horsepower blower.

Löf, who is also the executive vice-president of the Solaron Corporation, producers of solar air-heating systems, sees the main deterrent to widespread use of solar energy at the present time as the high capital cost of a good system. An effective system that requires little maintenance would cost between $4,000 and $5,000 for the hardware and another $2,000 for the average

Dr. and Mrs. Löf chat in their living room (left). In this room, they have entertained experts and dignitaries from around the world who have come to explore the uses of solar energy.

watt prevail, Löf calculates that the homeowner would save between $600 and $700 a year in heating bills, paying back the original investment in ten years or less, if power rates continue to rise. For the homeowner using oil, the expenses are about equal, the cost of solar equipment being about the same as the cost of fuel for the same period. Natural gas is the one fuel that solar energy cannot compete with in price. Gas continues to be the cheapest fuel—but it is also the most in danger of near-term depletion.

How does living in a solar house differ from living in a conventional house? To Dr. Löf and his wife a solar-heated house neither looks nor feels that different from a conventional house. Except, perhaps, for the flat roof, which leaks. "But flat roofs always leak," he adds. Does it change your lifestyle? "Yes," replied Mrs. Löf. "How else would we have all these scientists, politicians, and journalists visiting us from all over the world!"

Dr. Löf is currently working with the developing countries in utilizing solar energy. The greatest opportunities, in his view, are international. In underdeveloped nations like China, Pakistan, and India, solar power could be used for water desalination and crop drying as well as for domestic and industrial heating. Löf predicts that large corporations will become increasingly involved in solar technology, although, as he points out, it isn't easy to get a proprietary hold on solar power because the sun shines indiscriminately on everyone and everywhere.

installation. Increased demand and production could reduce the price of the hardware by a quarter or a third, he says, but distribution costs, factory overhead, and labor would remain the same, if not increase.

In some areas of the country, however, the investment is already economically sound. For areas where electricity rates of 6 cents per kilo-

Peter van Dresser

"I live in hope that a genuine psychic change may be operating on society as a whole and that the present gropings towards alternative systems are forerunners of a significant social change."

Peter van Dresser, director of Sun Dwellings Program in Santa Fe, New Mexico, is one of the granddaddies of environmental and natural-energy activists. His adobe house is one of the oldest continually operated solar-heated homes in the country. As a teacher, writer, and experimenter who was making solar hot water heaters in the 1930s, his contribution to the development of solar energy has been largely inspirational. A humanist searching for ways to improve the human condition, he has had a subtle though substantial impact on others.

"I don't like the term 'alternate technology,'" he says, "because it reflects the American hope that gadgets will solve everything. Even solar collectors and wind generators, useful as they are, cannot significantly help unless people are prepared to change their lifestyles and their thinking to fit into a more ecological way of living." To van Dresser, the technology is not an alternative; rather, it is appropriate, right for its time and place, and neither too wasteful nor too costly. Using what is at hand in the way it should be used is hardly a new idea but could have important implications if carried out on a wide scale.

As director of Sun Dwellings, van Dresser is currently working with a team on a prototype for a rural self-sufficient community in El Rito, New Mexico, that is based on the principles of natural-energy living. To him, it is the only answer to the urban problems of overpopulation and pollution. He believes in and is impressed by the serious groundwork being done by similar communities such as Ecotope in Washington (page 174), Farallones in California (page 178), and the New Alchemy Group in Massachusetts.

Van Dresser's adobe house in Santa Fe is an expression of his early commitment to environmental change. The building, which dates back to the 1930s, is a 500-square-foot one-story structure that he remodeled in 1958 to accommodate solar collectors on the roof. The total surface of 230 square feet of air-type solar collectors provides him with about 60 percent of his space heating needs. A wood-burning fireplace and a small gas heater supply the rest. The house has been considered a solar landmark for almost two decades now, and although the house may be a little the worse for wear, the solar system continues to function effectively.

This modest adobe brick house, not far from the downtown section of Santa Fe, was one of the earliest attempts to remodel, or retrofit, an existing house to use solar energy for its space heating and hot water. The house was designed in the 1930's out of low-cost, indigenous materials. Then, in 1958, Peter van Dresser raised the roof in two slanting sections at the front and back to accommodate the installation of solar collectors. The collector panels, made of ordinary plate glass over sheet metal boxes, are part of an air-to-rock solar heating system. The air heated by the sun in the solar collectors enters either one of two storage bins, filled with fist-sized rocks. One is located at the front of the house near the front row of collectors and another, larger, rock bin is located at the back. This system not only provides the house with its space heating but also supplies the hot water, employing an air-to-water heat exchanger. The hot water is stored in an insulated 30-gallon boiler that also has an electric immersion heater to boost the water temperature to the required 140 degrees Fahrenheit. Inside the house, the fireplace and a small gas heater are supplementary sources for the space heating to carry the house over a cloudy spell.

Henry Mathew

"It's nice to pick up free energy on a sunny day."

In the Pacific Northwest, Henry Mathew is a folk hero. In 1966, when anyone talking about solar heating might be considered a crackpot, Mathew built a conventional one-story, three-bedroom house in Coos Bay, Oregon, with a homemade flat plate solar collector on the roof. The house has been running on the sun ever since. His self-invented solar collector system has been the wonder of experts who sought him out during the energy crisis to pick his brains.

"There are two things we will always be indebted to Henry for," says John Reynolds, associate professor of architecture at the University of Oregon. "One, he actually built a solar house which actually works, and actually *in Oregon*—one of the worst places in the country." (The Oregon coast is well-known for its protracted overcast days, especially from December through February.) "And two, because he came up with the concept of a vertical collector/horizontal reflector combination, which is unique."

Experts say that for best wintertime performance, a solar collector should be placed at an angle to the ground equal to the latitude at which the house sits, plus 15 to 20 degrees. In Coos Bay, that would mean a very steep roof angled at 65 degrees. After some simple experiments, Mathew concluded that a 90-degree tilt (his is actually 82 degrees) with a reflective surface in front of it,

Henry Mathew's one-story home in Oregon is unusual only for the solar collectors which run along the roof ridge. The self-taught inventor of his own heating system stands outside and in his living room (below).

would work even better. That's what he put on his house—and he was right. Monitors by the University of Oregon during the winter of 1975 showed that 85 percent of the house's space heating came from his solar heating system.

Mathew is a carpenter and millwright by trade and a self-taught inventor. He got the idea for the solar system from an article in *Popular Mechanics* and started experimenting with window glass and water droplets set out in the sun. "I purposely built the house of standard construction and didn't overly insulate it to see what solar heating would do," he explained. He used only standard single-pane window glass despite winter temperatures as low as 17 degrees and a climate that includes hail and high wind velocities reaching up to 100 miles per hour.

He used only available, low-cost materials to build the solar collector and the 8,000-gallon water tank buried beneath the house. It took him three months, working all alone, and another five weeks to build the heat storage tank. The ordinary kitchen-type aluminum foil with which he lined the flat plate collector is still in use. Seven years later, Mathew added another collector, two-thirds the size of the original one and put it 65 feet away from the house in the backyard, and plugged it into the existing system. Up until then, he got 75 percent of all his heat from the sun. Now he gets almost all of his heating needs from the sun.

Grass-roots logic, the sort that many architects ignore but that modern-day mountain men like Mathew live by, guided him to put the living room and kitchen on the south side of the house and to shade that side with a long roof overhang. From November to January, the reflector/collector operates at full tilt, when the sun's rays are deflected to the collector plate. By April, however, as the sun moves higher in the sky, the reflector stops contributing, thus preventing the collector from overheating under the June-to-August sun.

Several years ago, Mathew built a second solar collector and placed it in his backyard about 65 feet behind the house. This free-standing unit is similar in design to the collectors mounted on his roof. That design is of special interest because of the reflector shield that Mathew placed below the face of the solar collectors. This aluminum foil-covered panel reflects additional radiation back toward the collectors' glass face and boosts its efficiency. In Oregon, known for its long cloudy periods, this added feature is an important factor in the success of Mathew's solar heating system.

Mathew's cost for the original system was under $1,000 with modifications, and the newer collector doubled his investment to $2,000. That excludes his own time and labor. He estimated that it would cost about twice as much to build today. As to repairs, he said, "Since 1967, windstorms have broken three of the 20-by-30-inch glass collector panes costing $2 each. I had to replace a damper motor that ran perfectly for four or five years, and it cost me 50 cents to replace the packing in the pump. I have never repainted or washed the collector panes, which are

ordinary window glass." Because the roof collector was giving only 75 percent of the winter heating, he decided to add the smaller collector for more efficiency. "It's much more comfortable in the house as you get close to 100 percent," he says. During the cloudy winter period, his electricity bill runs to $5 per month compared to $80 or $90 for the conventional electrically heated house in the area. "An oil-heated house would be even more," he said. "In Oregon, where we have hydro-electric power, electricity is cheaper than oil."

Every designer likes his own ideas best, and Mathew prefers his solar design to others. (He sells plans of his collector system for $10 by mail: Rt. 3, Box 768, Coos Bay, Oregon 97420.) But he is continually experimenting, trying other approaches, and is especially intrigued by the use of parabolic reflectors. One real advance, he believes, is the use of the solar greenhouse. Because of the world shortage of energy, he predicts that more and more people will turn to solar heating. "It's nice to pick up free energy on a sunny day," he says. "I expect that my children will live in solar houses in the near future."

Steve Baer

"It's not much different than living in any other kind of house."

Zomeworks, Inc., an enterprise that makes and sells solar hardware and is situated on the outskirts of Albuquerque, New Mexico, attracts solar enthusiasts like a magnet. Its founder, owner, and guru, Steve Baer, wishes it weren't so. Baer hates crowds, big "anything," (especially big business), and distraction from what really intrigues him: tensile structures and thermodynamics. To him, the two are interrelated, and the way he deals with them is best shown by his own home, a cluster of ten-sided rooms connected by doorways that he calls "zomes."

In the land of adobe building, Steve Baer's house is an anomaly. Corrales is the one section of Albuquerque that prides itself on its old adobe character (the rest of the town has gone the wood-frame route of the typical American suburb). There, perched on a sandhill, is the Baer homestead, a futuristic dome cluster glistening in the sun. The surface of the zomes is industrial sheet metal insulated with polyurethane foam. Solar heat is trapped in a south-facing wall consisting of 55-gallon barrels stacked behind plate glass windows.

The south walls of four of the zomes, which comprise the living area, are equipped with 10-by-10-foot windows of single-strength glass. Directly behind the glass panes are stacks of oil drums holding 20 tons of water in all. The south-facing ends of the drums are painted black, which is the most heat-absorbent color. All day long, the sun heats the water in the barrels. To prevent this heat from escaping at night, Baer devised flat, insulating covers of aluminum for the windows. At night, these insulating covers are hand-cranked to close and the hot water in the barrels radiates heat into the room. During the day, how-

Steve Baer's concept for his house outside of Albuquerque is one of the most unusual of contemporary alternate energy designs. The building consists of a curved chain of 4 main units, called zomes, each of which is connected by doorways so air can circulate through them. Most of the zomes are pierced by skylights that are covered by movable insulating skylids. These can be seen in the Baer dining room (above right) and in one of the bedrooms (lower right).

ever, the insulated panels lie flat on the ground, acting as crude mirrors to reflect additional solar radiation onto the barrel walls.

The process works in reverse to cool the house in summer. The insulated covers stay closed on hot days and are opened at night. Cool night air flows past the barrels, lowering the temperature of the water-filled barrels. With the insulated panels closed during the day, the cool barrels keep the interiors from overheating, providing the house with natural air conditioning. Baer claims that the rooms can be kept at 80 degrees even when the outside temperature reaches 100 degrees. Although they block the view, the drum walls are quite attractive inside the house. They look like an architectural screen with star-shaped patterns of light in the spaces between the drums.

While the drum wall heats most of the house,

The skylids, seen in the dining area (above), operate automatically to open or close. Attached to the edges of the skylids, or louvers, are tubes of Freon, which is sensitive to radiant heat. Natural thermostats, the Freon tubes control the indoor temperatures by monitoring the angles of the skylids. Baer's windmill (right) pumps water for his house and those of his two neighbors.

there are other nonmechanical solar heat catchers. In the kitchen, Baer devised large skylights covered by a clear plastic dome. These are fitted with "skylids," which are insulated louvers that open and close automatically depending upon what the sun is doing outside. Freon-filled tubes are attached to the louvers and act as sensors to the radiant heat, a natural thermostat controlling the opening and closing of the louvers. Such solutions— as few moving parts as possible— are Baer's forte.

Steve Baer is a zealot when it comes to wasteful mechanics and use of materials. His personal philosophy on solar technology is that it should be easy to operate and maintain. He is a product of the recycling movement of the late 1960s and started a commune, called "Drop City," in the hills of Colorado, where a lot of his ideas generated real innovations. It was there that Baer invented

The back of the zomes, and an outdoor patio, is seen above. Audrey Baer looks over the vegetable crop in the greenhouse.

the first zomes. The basic skeleton was a wood-framed dome. Baer and friends went to the nearest junkyard and hacked out triangles of steel from the tops of car bodies to cover the domes. However, the zomes leaked, and that gave the commune its name. Many Baer-devised words have since passed into the solar vocabulary: zomes, skylids, night walls, bead walls, and drum walls.

Hot water for the Baer house is supplied by a flat plate water-type collector system. A windmill outside the house pumps the water for Baer's home and for that of his two neighbors, both of whom built their own solar houses.

Baer lives with his wife, Holly, and their two children. Since its completion the house has required minimal maintenance. There have been only two leaks in the water drums, and these occurred in the ones sealed with zinc rather than those with steel bungs. Baer's fourteen-year-old daughter, Audrey, finds it a chore for her and her brother to crank up the window covers at night, but "otherwise it's not much different than living in any other kind of house," she said. "And it's certainly better than the bus we lived in while the house was being built."

Baer's house, unlike those which utilize mechanical solar collectors, is a completely "passive" solar design. Instead of using technological hardware to collect and store the sun's heat, the zomes' interior south-facing walls consist of water-filled oil drums stacked in front of large windows (right). The stacked oil drums create the effect of an architectural screen in the Baer living room. The Baers furnished their living room with handsome native designs such as their Navaho rugs on the floor as well as Indian coverings for the sofa. In the background, one of the dividing walls between the zomes is covered with book shelves.

Paul Davis

"I can tell when there are clouds at night without opening my eyes."

When Paul Davis, a professor of English at the University of New Mexico, bought two acres next door to solar designer Steve Baer in Corrales, New Mexico, he gained a neighbor, a mentor, and a source for his water supply. (Baer's windmill has the capacity to pump water to the two neighboring houses.) Davis wanted to build a solar house, and Baer suggested he choose adobe as the building material because of its natural insulating properties. Davis complied even though he had never worked in masonry and planned to do all the work himself. He ended up taking a course in adobe building at the local community college to learn how to work with the material.

Davis fitted his two-level house into a south-facing hillside. The lower level has 600 square feet of living space, and a loft provides an additional 300 square feet for bedrooms. The 400 square feet of solar collectors, which supply both the house's space heating and hot water, are located on the south facade, directly beneath a porch running across the front of the building. The porch is shielded by a roof overhang.

The solar heating system is an air-to-rock type that is both simple and ingenious. Steve Baer, who designed it, describes the system as a "solar chimney" because of the way the design utilizes natural air convection. The 12-foot-high by 36-foot-long area of sloping collectors is situated below the house. The heat storage area, a bin holding 45 tons of fist-sized rocks, is situated behind the collectors, directly beneath the floor of the house's living area. Air vents introduce air at the bottom of the collector where it is warmed and then circulated upward by natural convection. This warmed air is admitted into the house from the rock bin through registers in the floor (see diagram). The floor registers are manually operated, usually twice a day, to control the flow of warm air.

There are other design features to augment the solar heating system. For instance, the roof of the porch slides back in winter to expose the living room windows to the sun. A row of clerestory win-

The solar collectors rising out of the ground dominate the front facade of the Paul Davis house in New Mexico. A porch sits over the collectors. The projecting posts (above) support roof panels that can be slid over the beams to shade the living room windows from the hot summer sun.

Steve Baer calls the solar heating system he designed for the Davis house (right) a "solar chimney." It consists of a 12-by-36 foot array of collectors, which are boxes holding five layers of black-painted metal mesh with air spaces in between and enclosed by a glass front. Air enters the bottom of the collectors and rises up by natural convection to flow into the rock storage bin. The bin sits directly behind the collectors and beneath a part of the house's floor. Floor registers admit the heated air from the bin into the house. Flaps on the ducts regulate the flow.

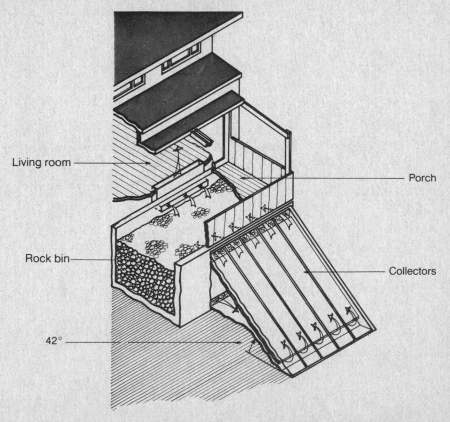

Living room

Porch

Rock bin

Collectors

42°

dows over the fixed glass wall of the south side of the house opens for ventilation during the summer months.

When Paul, his wife, Mary, and their two children moved in, they found the house almost unbearable. Even though the collectors were operating perfectly, the rooms were cold and damp. "I cursed Zeus because the sun didn't come up," Davis recalls of that first winter. "I had no faith—and studied lots of ads for furnaces."

Gradually, it dawned on Davis that the collectors' heat was just drying up the excess moisture in the ground surrounding the rock storage bed. Once the ground was dry, the solar system worked efficiently, providing about 75 percent of the building's heat needs. The Davises have a wood-burning fireplace for supplementary heat when the nights get chilly, which isn't too often. They rarely need more than a cord of wood for the winter months. Because Davis did all of the work himself, the house cost about $12 per square foot. The solar equipment came to another $3,000 to $4,000.

From the beginning, Steve Baer steered Davis away from complex solar hardware and mechanical devices and toward those that work with natural forces. The thermostat control for the vents on the floor registers leading up from the rock bin is a perfect example. The vents are controlled by a pull chain strung with colored beads. Each color signifies a different temperature gauge. So, whatever bead is caught in the hook tells how much heat the house is getting. "It's just a lot nicer than throwing a switch or fiddling with a dial," in Baer's view.

After that dubious housewarming, Paul Davis has subsequently undergone an almost spiritual transformation about living naturally. "You feel vulnerable at first. But then you begin to sense your body as a radiator. You get a sense of being more in touch with nature, not cut off from it. A house like this one becomes an extension of your body. Now I'm so in tune with the environment that I can tell when there are clouds at night without opening my eyes."

The Davises' son has a bedroom on a loft in the house (above left). The professor uses the crawl space (above) behind the collectors as a library to store his books.

Everett Barber

"This is primal and gives you a feeling of control over your destiny."

Solar consultant Everett Barber, who is an associate professor of environmental technology at Yale University and lives in Guilford, Connecticut, posed himself a problem: He wanted an energy-conscious house for a middle-income family of five that was "designed by an architect, built by a builder, and financed by a bank." Because Barber had been designing solar systems and had started a business called Sunworks (it has since been sold), solar energy was very much a part of the program.

"Working toward solar energy, I had so many design criteria," he says, "that the house practically designed itself." The house is a maze of interrelated systems, some mechanical, others structural and nonmechanical, that work to heat the house and its hot water. A checklist of the original design requirements reads as follows: (1) house to face south, (2) roof large enough for 400 square feet of water-type collectors angled at 57 degrees, (3) little or no glass on the north side, (4) concrete block for thermal mass, (5) polyurethane foam to insulate the concrete block on the outside for the best heat retention, (6) fireplace near the solar water storage tank (which is in the living room), (7) a belvedere (a vent tower at the top of the house), and (8) roof overhangs for sun control. Architects Charles Moore and Richard Oliver helped to incorporate all of the features he required into the design.

The house, Barber says, is first of all a home, but the technology that runs it makes a strong statement. The solar collectors are designed to feed heat into a 2,000-gallon water storage tank placed in the living room. "It's just inside the entry so that all who enter are confronted by the size of the container needed to keep the house warm. Ideally," Barber explains, "it gives some sense of scale to the amount of heat we have to store to sustain our lifestyle."

Barber has worked out an ingenious series of systems that are designed like links in a chain to work in concert. There are three levels of heat storage built into the house: the solar roof collectors that drop their heat into the 2,000-gallon

Ev Barber (left) stands in front of his new home. The design of the house incorporates many features derived from energy-conscious logic. The roof is pitched to give the as-yet-to-be-installed solar collectors the proper slant. Windows on the north are purposely small and overhangs protect them from wind and sun. Others (above), project out at angles from the house to capture a slice of sunlight.

Everett Barber has worked out an ingenious series of energy-saving ideas that are designed like links in a chain to work in concert (below). Three primary systems of heat storage are built into the plan for the house: (1) a water-type solar roof collector that connects to a 2,000 gallon free-standing heat storage tank in the living room, (2) a 50-gallon oil-fired hot water heater (whose water can be preheated by the solar collectors) that also acts as a space heater, and (3) by pulling heat via fans through ducts from the top of the house down to the stone bed.

Little heat in the house is wasted. The huge solar water storage tank is fitted with a coil that hooks up to the fireplace. Water circulated through it is heated by the fire in the hearth and then returned to the tank. One of the air ducts in the rock bed hooks up to the clothes dryer, supplying it with preheated air. In summer a belvedere with an exhaust fan expels heat from inside the house for natural cooling.

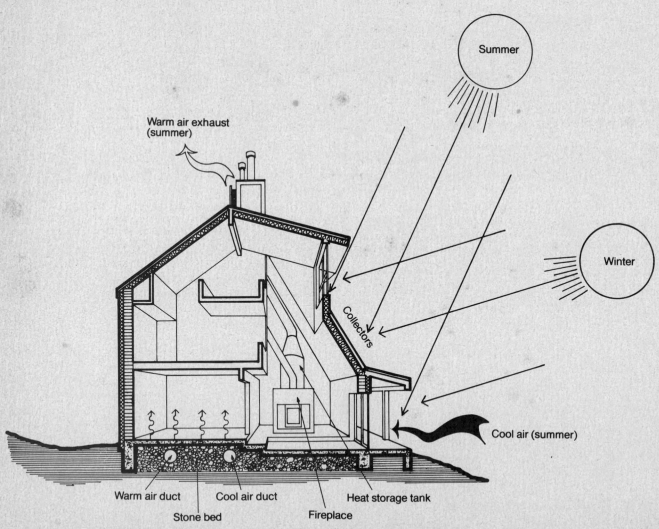

Summer

Winter

Collectors

Warm air exhaust (summer)

Cool air (summer)

Warm air duct   Cool air duct   Heat storage tank

Stone bed   Fireplace

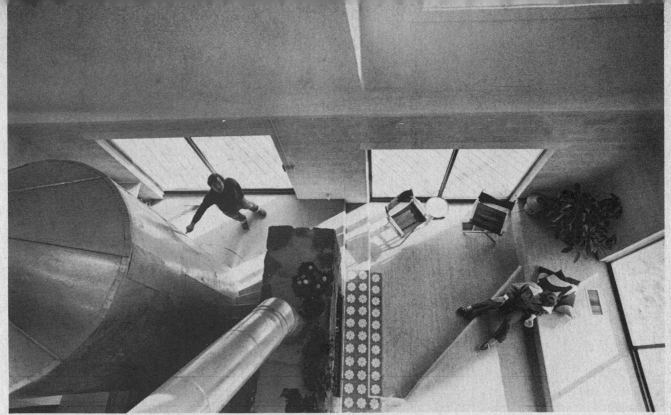

The 2,000-gallon tank that is the main reservoir for the sun-heated water sits right in the middle of the Barbers' living room. It is located behind the large fireplace, seen from above. The changing floor level acts to invite use as seating platforms.

water storage tank, a 50-gallon oil-fired hot water heater, and a rock bed that lies beneath the ground floor's concrete slab. Each contributes to the overall space heating to provide the house with 70 percent of its winter heat needs.

Warm air can be circulated or retrieved at several points: by a blower circulating it up from the rock storage bed, by circulating it around the air space or "sleeve" of corrugated metal surrounding the water storage tank, or by pulling it via fans through ducts down from the top of the house to the rock storage bed.

When Barber erects the two windmills he plans to put into operation, they will provide the power to run the house appliances. He believes that the windmills can eventually supply 80 percent of his electricity. He also plans to install a special system to retrieve the "gray water" from sinks and showers for toilet flushing.

Barber admits that the plans for the house have become more expensive than he anticipated. He estimated that the 1,300-square-foot house, with

the special energy retrieval systems, would cost around $46,000; it will turn out to be closer to $65,000. About $10,000 went for the custom-designed and -built storage tank, heating systems, solar collectors, and monitoring controls. But most of the extra expenditures were due to a rash of bad luck and construction mix-ups rather than to the the design of the system.

The experience, while often painful, was important to Ev Barber. "I wanted to set an example that others could learn from, and I think there will be a lot of positive material here." His wife, Gingee, adds, "You're not overpowered by the technology. I even like living with the water tank. The house is sassy, jaunty, self-assured."

Barber's goal is to reduce the building's energy requirement to next to nothing. "The more you get involved with passive solutions, the less dependent you are on the centralized society. This is primal and gives you a feeling of control over your destiny."

David Wright

"In the next ten years the architectural landscape of this country will change radically."

Environmental architect David Wright developed a simple way to heat a house by the sun that has worked in different regions and different climates. A Berkeley-educated ex-Peace Corps member, Wright was one of the original members of Sun Mountain Design, in Santa Fe, New Mexico, a nonprofit group of engineers, builders, and architects involved in solar-tempered design. They approached land use, development, design, and research synergistically, learning from their various disciplines. David, like the others, prefers nonmechanical, sun-heated houses to those with complicated systems involving collectors, storage, and circulation systems.

His own house on the outskirts of Santa Fe, in the foothills of the Sangre de Cristo Mountains, is a prototype of the nonmechanical structures he advocates. The design is straightforward. In fact, one might even question the use of the term "solar house." The only visible hardware is a small separate solar collector that stands several yards from the house on the south slope. It supplies the house with hot water.

In appearance, the house blends harmoniously with the native New Mexican architecture. It uses adobe brick, and the roof overhang echoes the traditional *vigas*, or roof beams, that extend out through the walls of old adobe houses. Its inspiration goes even farther back—to the twelfth-century pueblo dwellings at Chaco Canyon, considered by many to be America's first solar-heated habitations on a grand scale. At Chaco Canyon, the multifamily structures that were archetypal apartment buildings to house a whole community, were built in an arc. The windows and doorways faced south, into the sun, while the backs of the pueblos were shielded by the hillside, giving them protection from northern winds.

The Wright house reflects that same design. From a bird's-eye view, it is shaped like a semicircle with a flat front. The curved walls are 14-inch-thick adobe brick with 2 more inches of polyurethane insulation covered by a thick layer of stucco. The flat front, facing south, is a two-story-high window wall made up of double-glazed

Although the David Wright house (left) is small in size, the two-story-high windows make the interiors appear very spacious (above). The deep roof overhang on the outside shields the windows from the excesses of the summer sun. The house itself is an example of passive solar design, although there is a small, separate solar water-type collector that supplies the house with its hot water. It sits in a free-standing structural frame a few feet from the front of the house.

59

Basic, energy-saving concepts lay behind architect David Wright's design (below). The 14-inch thick adobe brick walls and foundation are covered with 2-inch thick layers of polyurethane insulation. Roof overhangs that protect the windows in summer allow the sun's rays to penetrate the interiors in winter all the way to the back wall. The north side of the house is protected by an earth berm. Another special design feature of the house are the insulated shutters that are operated manually to close over the windows at night, trapping the sun's heat inside. Architect David Wright stands on the second-floor balcony of his house (top right). The balcony space serves as both his office and the master bedroom. Both areas have a view of the distant mountains through the tall windows of the building. The kitchen is below the balcony (below right). It is separated from the living area by a serving counter. Mrs. Wright's loom is set up more or less permanently.

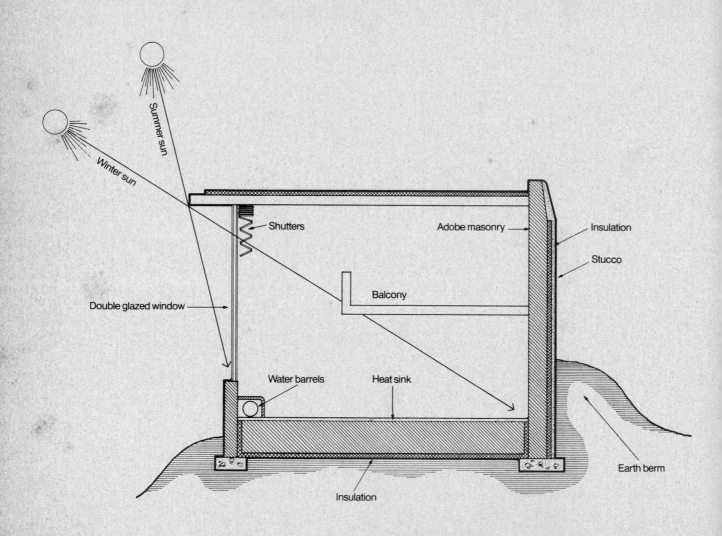

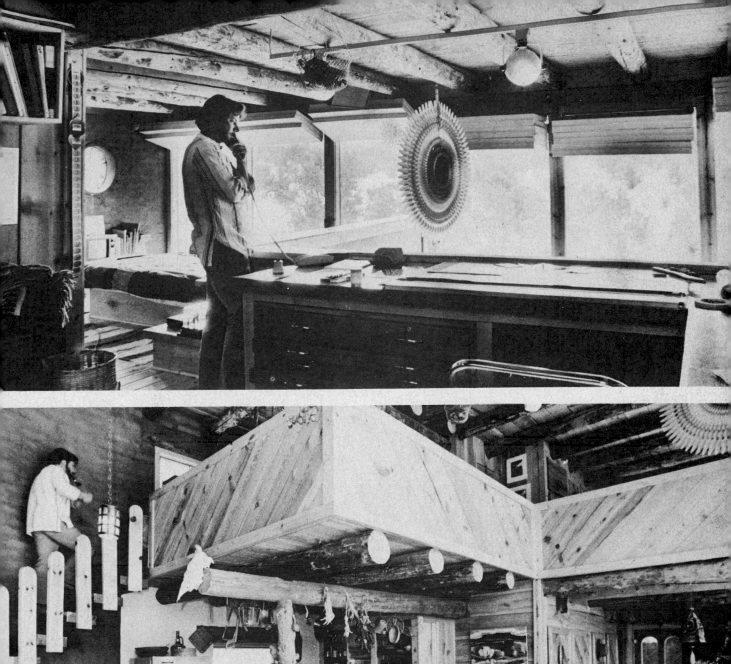

sliding doors. An overhang shields the windows from the hottest summer sun. In contrast to the front, the three remaining sides of the house are surrounded by an earth bank and broken only by a few small windows set high up to act as vents. On the east, the main entry door is protected by a vestibule that creates an air trap so warm house air can't escape each time the door is opened.

David, with his wife, Barbara, built the house almost single-handedly with some subcontracting for electrical and plumbing work and a couple of part-time crews who worked two-week stints. The house took them less than six months to complete and cost the couple around $13,000, not counting their own labor. The interior is basically a two-story-high room with a balcony. The lower level has a relaxed cabin atmosphere and is a congregating point to enjoy the view of the Sangre de Cristo Mountains (named "Blood of Christ" for their spectacular blood-red sunsets). Although the house is small, the window wall gives the interior a feeling of generous space.

David Wright's concept of a solar "heat sink," such as the one they adopted in this house, was popular in the late 1930s. Houses were marketed and sold as "solar houses," but they never adequately solved the basic problem: what to do with the excess heat during the day and how to stem the heat loss at night. (Night losses usually exceed the daily heat gains.) Superior insulation and the thermal building mass of adobe were Wright's solution to that problem. To augment the natural insulation provided by the adobe walls, fifteen 50-gallon water-filled oil drums, buried beneath the living room window, soak up the sun's warmth. Water holds about four times as much heat as adobe, and also absorbs it and gives it off faster. To further reduce heat loss at night, accordion-fold shutters made of canvas and 2-inch polyurethane panels are raised and lowered by a hand-operated crank and pulley to cover the vast expanse of the window wall at night.

Since completion, the house has required practically no maintenance. The Wrights found that space heating based on the concept of thermal lag, follows natural rhythms and puts the body's metabolism in tune with it. "The body heats up and cools down gradually with the building," David explains. "Unlike convective heat, where you're always standing in a draft of hot or cold air, radiant heat is natural, steady, and follows the body's natural metabolism and doesn't give the system the jolts of convected heat. It's more comfortable." During the winter months the Wrights found that the house stores about five days' worth of heat, enough to carry through an average cloudy period in New Mexico. For auxiliary heat, they have a wood-burning Franklin stove, which uses less than a cord of wood a year.

Because houses like his are so economical to construct, operate, and maintain, Wright sees the architectural landscape of this country changing radically to conform to these principles in the next ten years. "Solar and climatic design is the first major innovation in architecture since balloon framing," he says. Balloon framing, the basic 16-inch-stud-on-center construction, is a mainstay of the building industry and came into use during the 1890s following the Chicago fire. In view of today's energy needs, balloon framing is wasteful and obsolete because, "people will move more into the earth, blended into the ground, out of function and need; buildings will face south to take advantage of the sun's benefits." Wright practices what he preaches. The house he is now building in Sea Ranch, California, is partially buried.

The Wrights relax on the long banco *beneath the living room windows. The bench augments the room's furnishings and is an especially delightful place from which to sit and enjoy the view, but it performs an even more important function. Embedded inside the adobe-built bench are water-filled oil drums that store the sun-generated heat.*

Wayne Nichols

"Your (solar) house is your own energy company."

The Wayne Nicholses' house in Santa Fe doesn't look all that different from those of their neighbors. It's made of adobe brick and has a banked side patio: there's a familiarity about the outline and form. The only unusual feature is the steeply pitched roof that is faced with reflective glass panels. The panels are the solar collectors which supply the house with heat and also serve to preheat the hot water.

The house looks conventional on purpose. Wayne Nichols is an enlightened developer, who believes that the world is ready for solar-heated houses. He and his wife, Susan, own CommuniCo, a small real estate development firm which specializes in building custom solar homes that sell for $80,000 to $100,000. They are in the process of building an environmental community, 6 miles south of Santa Fe, called First Village. Starting with four houses, each on 5 acres of land, the houses will be clustered around a central plaza and

Wayne Nichols' house combines the new technology of solar hardware with the charm of traditional Southwest features. The 550 square feet of air-type solar collectors on the south-facing roof (left) blend nicely with the adobe walls. Inside (above), Nichols retained the custom of an adobe fireplace and exposed overhead beams, lending charm to the room.

surrounded by 15 acres of undisturbed landscape.

Their own home is the model for the project. It was built by Wayne, Susan, and a small team of assistants, who will be able to go out and build other solar structures based on the skills they have learned. Wayne was part of the construction crew, and rather than work from set drawings, he made decisions during the construction process. "The owner involvement enabled a flow of ideas that made the building process very fluid," his wife says. "Everyone who worked on it had a real feeling of involvement with the house."

As developers catering to a conservative market, the Nicholses realized they had to pay special attention to the division of the interior spaces of a solar house. Designing around the solar collectors and the heat storage bins requires adaptations not encountered in an ordinary house. The collector hardware surface is equal in size to one-third the 1,800-square footage of the interior spaces, for instance, and they were designing for an average family's needs. "A master bedroom and one large living space for cooking, eating, and being together," Susan explained, "plus smaller private spaces for each of the five of us." That prompted them to place the living area at the front of the house for direct southern sun, tucking private spaces—three sleeping lofts—under the steep roof of the collector. "By doing that we gained another 400 square feet of floor space," Susan says. "And it

During the winter months, the patio is converted into a plastic sheet-covered greenhouse (top left and above). Like many solar energy enthusiasts, Susan and Wayne Nichols are down-to-earth and informal. In the living room (left), there is a free-form adobe fireplace near the study and music area where the family likes to congregate.

Wayne Nichols placed three bedroom lofts underneath the steep roof backing up to the solar collectors. The bedroom lofts are pleasantly rustic, in keeping with the character of the adobe architecture. Logs, stripped of bark, form the banister separating the lofts from below, The sloped roof is faced with rough-sawn planks that act as headboards.

gave each of our three kids a private room, each heated naturally by air convection."

The Nicholses also made efficient use of the space adjoining the rock storage bin (which holds 34 tons of rocks and is buried under the floor in the back, or north, of the house) by converting it into a sauna. "We needed access to the bin and had to construct a small cellar next to it. By opening the door to the storage bin, the sauna air is preheated. We use less electricity to boost the sauna to the desired 170 degrees."

Earth is good, cheap insulation, so the Nicholses sunk the house 4 feet underground, and where they didn't dig they banked with earth. That lowered the roof height of the solar collectors relative to the neighboring houses. It was also a cost saver, because the buried portion of the house is cement block, which is cheaper than adobe brick. The cement block and adobe brick are sheathed in 2 inches of polystyrene insulation, and then stuccoed. The north, east, and west walls are wood two-by-six frame construction insulated with 6 inches of fiberglass batts. The frame construction is a compromise, because building adobe brick walls to support the collector would have been expensive.

In winter, the Nicholses cover the patio area, just off the kitchen, with a double wall of plastic, converting it into a greenhouse. It provides vegetables and a thermal barrier for the sliding glass doors of the house. A 400-gallon pool in the greenhouse acts as an additional heat source for the greenhouse during winter nights.

Wayne claims that it's easy to build a solar heating system yourself. "Ten thousand dollars can provide a total air-to-rock system for a 2,000-square-foot house," he says. "Simpler systems cost less. If you don't aim for 100-percent efficiency, you can do a lot by sinking the house under ground, as we did, then combining active and passive systems to create radiant heat surfaces."

While the Nicholses were working on the house in winter, before the solar collector was hooked up, they found that the insulation gave the house a "thermos-bottle effect." With daily solar build-up

and three fireplaces, the interior temperature was comfortable even *without* the collector. And on cold nights, the house temperature never fell below 48 degrees. The backup electrical heating equipment, using the same ducts as the solar system, supplies only 20 percent of the heating energy needed for the winter months.

Lifestyles change in a solar house, say the Nicholses—for the better. "Your house is your own energy company," says Susan. "It's very different from conventional living. It's more like sailing. You trim, you adjust. You conserve. You capture your heat—vent the dryer indoors, the stove, the sauna. Solar living puts you back in touch with the rhythms of nature—watching the sun, the clouds. Emotionally, that's a good place to get back to. If we had a whole community that felt that way, look what it would do toward reaching self-sufficiency naturally!"

Developers have been the key to this country's growth for the past twenty years. People like Wayne Nichols may steer the housing market toward natural energy. "If you can't start at the inner city, which is the core of the problem, you try New Mexico first," he says. "If you achieve an evolutionary flash, if enough people adopt the model, the system regenerates itself. It's beginning to happen here and in other communities, like Berkeley and Cambridge, and in the countryside in Oregon, Vermont, and Massachusetts. Solar and natural energy are the keys to survival."

Hal Migel

"It's an experimental and experiential building that will change as we go along."

Hal Migel, a sculptor by training and a designer-builder by trade, describes his house in the hills of Tesuque, New Mexico, as a hybrid. It integrates ideas from two schools of thought on indirect, or passive, solar design. His adobe brick structure is a thick thermal envelope that builds up and stores the sun's heat. It incorporates a greenhouse on the south as the main solar heat collector. A secondary collector is an 18-inch-thick wall that separates the greenhouse from the living room and works on the principle of a Trombe wall.

In the Migel house, the greenhouse interior is the cavity that collects the solar-heated air. The heated air is conducted into the living room when the windows and doors are opened. The masonry wall itself also builds up solar heat, which is radiated into the living room at night.

Because the greenhouse is the main solar heat reservoir, its foundation is extra thick. A 6-foot-deep rock bed runs the perimeter of the room; floors are adobe brick. A central fan circulates the air from five intake points near the ground, through the rock bed, and into the greenhouse.

Hal, his wife, and the sometimes help from a crew of five took nine months to complete the house. The family built it out of mostly low-cost indigenous materials. The greenhouse, for instance, has a redwood frame covered with two layers of plastic sheeting that create an air cushion. The "pillow wall" is a cheap, effective insulator, but it degenerates quickly. The Migels allow it to deteriorate over the winter, then rip it off in summer and turn the greenhouse into an outdoor patio. In winter it's a second living room and is hung with exotic plants, and the whole family uses it as a sun porch.

"It's an experimental and experiential building that will change as we go along," says Hal Migel.

The Migel homestead in New Mexico is a passive solar heated house. Its adventurous design, combines two giant adobe drums that contrast with the steep roof of the greenhouse at the left. The experimental design perhaps can be attributed to the owner's training as a sculptor. Hal Migel built the house himself with the help of a crew of five.

The Migel family and friends gravitate naturally to the pleasant atmosphere of the greenhouse (left), especially in winter. In summer, the plastic sheeting is removed and the room becomes an outdoor patio. The hexagonal window at the back of the house (above) is another of the owner's sculptural flourishes.

Because of his tight budget, compromises had to be made that he would like to correct eventually. The 2,100-square-foot building cost about $20 per square foot—"excluding the donation of my wife's and my time in construction," he adds. The greenhouse addition proved less effective than anticipated, and Migel says he plans to open up the living spaces of the house more directly to the greenhouse. When the budget allows, he will also replace the greenhouse plastic sheeting with permanent tempered-glass panels. At present, there isn't enough money to operate the temperature sensors that Migel installed to keep tabs on how well the building functions as a solar habitation.

The fuel bill is the ultimate indicator of how well a solar building works, and here the Migels have no serious complaints. They estimate that they save about $500 in heating bills each winter.

But, as Hal Migel points out prophetically, "This could mean a savings of $2,000 annually a decade from now.

"We can live at lower air temperatures when the solid mass of the building is warm. And with the higher humidity from the plants in the greenhouse, the body feels comfortable at lower air temperatures," Migel says. One of the principles of solar living is to insulate the body, and many people living in solar houses wear vests in winter as a matter of course. Many say that their metabolism changes so that they now find they feel sleepy in conventionally heated houses. When the temperature at the Migel household drops below 63 degrees, an auxiliary propane-gas-fired heater with room air registers begins to operate. There is also a traditional adobe brick fireplace in the west wall of the living room.

Karen Terry

"It's the morality of the design of the house that's so important."

Karen Terry's solar house is compact, a mere 864 square feet, yet it looks and lives like a much bigger house. It was designed by architect David Wright of the Sun Mountain Design group (his house is shown on page 58), and it uses the same energy-saving principles. The fabric of the house—the thick, well-insulated adobe brick walls and floors, the south-facing windows, the water-filled drums buried in walls where the sun shines on them—are all refinements of the Wright house. The front windows set in four stepped banks face south, while the north side is buried and banked into the back of a hill. Terry's house is heated exclusively by direct solar gain. It has no complicated solar hardware or collectors, or air circulation or storage systems. The thick exterior walls are baked by the sun, absorb the heat, and then radiate it back into the interiors at night. It operates by means of thermal lag—that is, the time it takes for equalization of the inside and outside temperatures.

That thermal lag, according to Karen Terry, a woodworker-potter, is why the house is so attuned to nature. "Living in a solar house is a whole new

Banks of windows stepping up a Santa Fe hillside echo the stepped levels inside the Karen Terry house. From within (above), the south-facing angled windows act as skylights to tap sunlight for solar heat.

75

awareness, another dimension," she says. I have the comfort of a house with the serenity of being outdoors—protected, yet tuned into it. I can lie in bed and see the sun come up and, at night, watch the stars. It's like living on a boat."

Karen is a free spirit who lives in balance with her environment. She lived on a 40-foot fishing boat in Alaska just before coming back to New Mexico, where her family owned some land. She visited the earth-covered Indian dwellings of Chaco Canyon, and they inspired her to plan her own solar-heated pueblo. Then she met David Wright of the Sun Mountain group and the plans expanded into a full-scale house that, although she had no previous building experience, she decided to build on her own. Tom Brady, an experienced adobe construction worker, showed her how to heft and lay the 30-pound adobe bricks. During construction she lived on her 3-acre tract in a tepee.

Architect Wright freely admits that Karen came up with the house's handsome and unusual design. It has three levels inside: the lowest is the workshop, the middle is the kitchen-dining area, and the top level is the bedroom and bath. There are two wood-burning stoves, one on each of the two lower levels. The house is stepped to let air convect naturally from the lower to the higher levels. Karen, in turn, follows the temperature, working in the cool lower level, eating in the middle level, and sleeping in the warmer top level.

"You have to learn to live with daily temperature swings of 15 to 20 degrees," she explains. "On a winter day, it may get as high as 80 and as low as 60 degrees inside. You have to learn to live without an even 70 degrees, to work with the house." The windows and the stepped levels work in tandem with the house shell as a solar collector. Buried in the kitchen balcony wall are 1,000 gallons of water in 50-gallon drums. The skylight-windows (depending on which way you look at them; from below they are skylights, from eye level they're windows) are aimed at the water-filled drum walls so that the sun's rays miss the barrels during the summer but hit them in winter when the sun is lower in the sky.

A thick thermal exterior skin conserves the solar heat. The house is constructed out of adobe brick with 2-inch polystyrene panels, covered by adobe plaster. The floor is built up with a plastic sheet vapor barrier, 2 inches of styrofoam insulation, 2 feet of dirt, and finally a top surface of brick. The windows are all double-insulating glass. Karen plans to install shutters to control excessive heat buildup inside during the summer months.

Karen considers this her first real home in years. She spared no effort to get everything done the best way she could. "We avoided shortcuts, tried to make no mistakes with the construction, to do everything right. And we created a wonderful house. It is an enormous accomplishment, the best effort I ever made."

The house works well over the winter months, she claims, even during the coldest periods when outside temperatures drop into the low teens at night. "If there is no sun for several days," she says, "I use one or both of the wood-burning stoves. Someday I'll get a Norwegian stove to replace the homemade cut-off oil drum in the studio." (The Jøtul, a Norwegian stove, burns logs in an enclosed heat chamber and is highly efficient. One log lasts for hours, the stove radiating its warmth. In an ordinary open fireplace, a log is consumed in one-quarter of that time, and most of its heat is lost up the chimney.)

The house cost more than Terry planned, $28 a square foot, or one-third more than estimated—the result, she says, of careful workmanship and the site's inaccessibility. "With a passive system not much energy is expended, except for the petroleum used to make the insulation and the glass, which amortizes itself fast." If you look at insulation as an investment, that expense quickly amortizes itself. Karen Terry believes, "We all have to learn how to conserve energy. And it's the morality of the design of the house that's so important."

Karen Terry keeps the lowest level of the three-story house as her work studio. As a hidden heat retention feature, the circular adobe wall to the right of the staircase has water-filled oil drums embedded in it. Sun pouring in from the skylights hits the wall, heating up the water in the barrels, which in turn act as heat reservoirs.

Carolyn Allers

"As many people as possible should make use of the sun before the big corporations take it away from us."

Carolyn Allers believed in ecology, energy conservation, and organic gardening long before they became popular movements. She planned to put up a wind generator on her Colorado ranch back in the 1930s. Even though a long-time resident of Riverdale, New York, she felt most at home in the Rockies and moved out to Santa Fe once her daughter was grown.

Carolyn was the first official client of the Sun Mountain Design group in Santa Fe. Like all pioneers, she ended up learning along with them; some lessons were exhilarating, others painful and costly. She views her experience philosophically: "I inherited some money from an oil lease and am alleviating my guilt."

Allers's solar-heated house is unusual. It is a hundred-year-old log cabin, trucked 120 miles to its present site. Additions to it are a solar collector on the roof, a rock storage bed, and a greenhouse on the south-facing side. It was an early attempt to retrofit an existing structure into a combination greenhouse–solar–wind-power package.

Energy conservation starts with the ground you're on and the materials that are there. So, in 1972, when a friend, builder Ben Zeller, suggested that Carolyn move the old log cabin he was living in on a ranch near Raton, New Mexico, she took him up on it. The hand-hewn logs, notched and fastened with wood pegs, were in fine shape. Only the mortar was gone. The building was cheap and easy to move: Zeller dismantled it, carefully numbering each log with chalk, and shipped it off. The stack of logs sat on the new site through the winter. By spring all the numbers had washed off, and it was a nightmare to piece it back together.

The cabin's flat plate air-type collectors are part of the roof structure. They are oversized (432 square feet) for the small 650-square-foot cabin—to compensate for the low roof deflection. An electric fan circulates collector-heated air through ducts down to a rock storage bed under the house. Heated air moves up through wall ducts to the rooms. A greenhouse was added to the south side for additional warmth in the winter.

The rock storage bed, which holds 24 cubic yards of rocks, was purposely left uninsulated to leak solar heat through the floors of the cabin interior. A second solar collector on the carport roof heats the cabin's hot water supply. "I only take baths on sunny days," Mrs. Allers quips.

The forty-year-old wind generator she installed was phased out because there wasn't enough wind on the site to run it efficiently. This and other problems shot up the builder's bills for the natural-energy equipment from $3,000 to $15,000. Carolyn explained that the extra costs were as much the result of plain bad luck as the system's novelty. It took two shipments to truck the river rock for the rock storage bed up from Albuquer-

Carolyn Allers enjoys the rustic ambiance of this 100-year-old log cabin, which she had moved to its present site and then retrofitted for solar heating with roof-mounted collectors.

que, 60 miles away. The collectors had to be custom-cut on the site. A special polyurethane sheeting had to be purchased from New Hampshire to protect the collectors' glass from the sudden, violent summer hailstorms that are a frequent phenomenon in these parts. Because the first shipment got lost in transit, a second one had to be ordered. In 1972, not one of the electricians, plumbers, or carpenters was familiar with working with solar hardware.

Mrs. Allers was closely involved in the designing of many of
the features of the house, including the wrought-iron gate
(above) and staircase (below right) in the bedroom.

Mrs. Allers has good reason to be sour about solar technology, but she isn't. She loves the climate and the beautiful country, including her Dr. Strangelove view of the Los Alamos Scientific Laboratory, home of the atomic bomb, across the Rio Grande. "I feel part of the energy-conserving community, an energy pioneer," she says. "It's important to make this kind of statement and investment, especially here because the government is so heavily involved in dangerous nuclear development."

Then, too, the solar system frees her somewhat from the public utility's exploitation. The cabin's thick wood logs and specially insulated chinks are excellent natural insulators. The collector supplies 80 percent of her heat. Only after two or three cloudy days in a row in winter does she turn on the backup heat system. Hers is a gas furnace that uses the same ducts as the solar air collector system. The gas bills average about $6 per month from December through March, compared with about $3 per month in the summer. The cabin's wood-burning fireplace gets a lot of use, but then, blazing hearths are a social thing in New Mexico, lighted almost ritualistically as the sun goes down.

Mrs. Allers is a fervent proselytizer about natural-energy living. "I think the house is a work of art, and it fits the lifestyle I've always wanted. It's easy, comfortable, and much more in tune with nature. As many people as possible should make use of the sun before the big corporations take it away from us," she says. "They'll invent solar cells and panels, patent them, and then monopolize or suppress them."

The interiors of the cabin (left) resemble a cozy weekend hide-a-way. In the bedroom (below left), the niches between the logs are perfect for storing books.

Daniel Newman

"We must reinvent this kind of elemental structure for our own social and psychological survival."

Solar advocates talk passionately about the Indian cultures and their love of the land, of Chaco Canyon, Mesa Verde, and the pueblo dwellings that were early solar-heated habitations. Native American wisdom has a strong appeal for people like Daniel Newman, a painter, who after five years of intensive university teaching as professor of art and English at Rutgers, took a sabbatical and came to New Mexico. He and his wife, Sandra, a poet, sought a back-to-the-elements existence to get back in touch with nature and simple human values. Newman chose a house form that he could build himself, an octagonal hogan, an earth-covered Indian lodge but with an attached greenhouse to lend solar heat. He was attempting a prototype for a low-cost elemental structure. It cost under $10 a square foot, or roughly $4,000, to build near Cerrillos, which is only 15 miles from Santa Fe but so remote that it looks like a set for a Hollywood western.

Newman describes the hogan as "an inverted basket covered by a pot that hasn't been fired. The rain packs it, and the sun fires it." He built it with the help of a visiting student, and his family (which numbers seven children but usually includes only four) moved in four months later. Newman used the traditional "whirling log" roof technique, starting the spanning at 6 feet. The interior space is 14 feet high and 20 feet across. The hogan, on footings of local stone, is banked with earth to a thickness of 10 feet at the bottom, decreasing to 2 feet where the roof curves. A large skylight pierces the center of the building. The roof is a mixture of pumice and earth with only earth as the capping. A vapor barrier of stucco and asphalt paint protects the log walls from moisture.

"The fact that we used Navaho forms does not mean we want to live like Indians," says Newman. He perceives the building as highly symbolic, even mystical. "The six- or eight-sided forms are good to live in," he says. And the hogan gives a strong sense of "place" in the natural landscape. Outside is the prairie horizon of mountains, brush, and sky, and inside, the sense of shelter, through the

Rising out of the juniper-covered New Mexico landscape is Daniel and Sandra Newman's first hogan, a one-room dwelling that uses the earth for insulation in the tradition of the Navahos. The Newmans added to the basic Indian design by inserting skylights (top) to bring more daylight inside. The water from their well is stored in a conventional 800-gallon water tank (above).

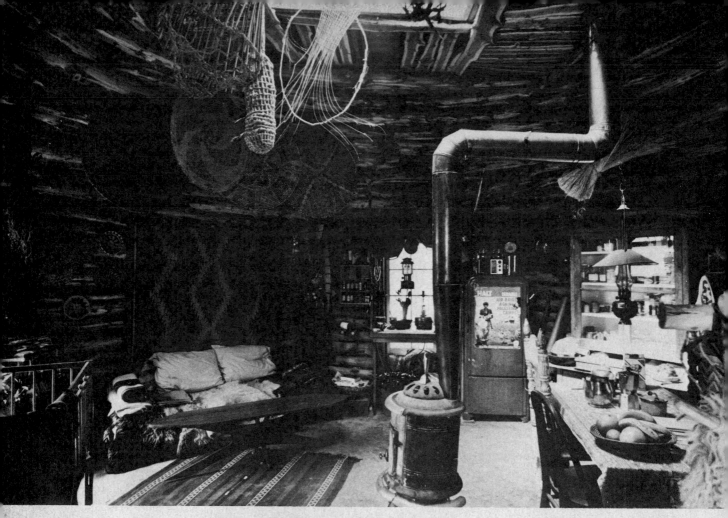

The hogan interior (above) is as snug in winter as it is cool in summer because of the extremely thick earth insulation. Logs form the interior surfaces of the walls and ceiling. The hogan is furnished like a rustic pioneer cabin and is heated by a wood-burning stove in the center. Sandra Newman is an expert basket weaver and the author of a book on the subject. Under a brush shelter near the hogan (right), she selects rushes for basket weaving. Daniel (far right) pauses in his building of a larger set of hogans nearby.

complex textures, the log walls, and the fireplace.

"It's a double dialectic," he says. "On the one hand, it uses the Indian traditions—the east-facing door and earth covering. It recalls the Hopi *kiva*, an enclosure based on the Indian legend that the tribe survived the world destruction by hiding underground in the earth's navel, and the *sipapu*, or hole of emergence, which signifies the act of re-creation." Although it is meant to look crude from the outside, "inside it's a surprise," Daniel Newman says. "It is very sophisticated." They use the greenhouse to grow flowers and vegetables. "It's an experiment, like any work of art," Newman explains.

Sandra was familiar with Indian cultures and lifestyles. She had studied with the Navaho and Pima Indians and from them learned basket weaving. She is the author of *Indian Basket Weaving* (Northland Press, 1974).

"We take so many things for granted," Daniel says. "The beauty of this existence, of doing everything for yourself, is that you begin with the very elemental things. For a time we had no water in the house. When the well was dug and we had water, we felt very grateful. We time our activities to the rhythms of the day, working and reading during daylight and often going to bed at dusk." At night they use a combination of candles and kerosene lamps.

The Newmans are building another hogan 300 yards away for their children. It is designed as a double hogan, two rooms each, about the size of the one they themselves live in, separated by an underground room with a kitchen-greenhouse-solar collector on top. They estimate that the cost of the 1,600-square-foot structure will be no more than $10,000. The greenhouse-cum-solar collector, they found, works very efficiently to heat a hogan, because of the superior insulating quality of the earth mass for heat storage. During an average winter they burn less than a cord of wood, their only auxiliary heat source.

"We must reinvent this kind of elemental structure for our own social and psychological survival," Daniel Newman believes, "not to mention the economic element at the center. But it's more than an ecological-economical problem. It's renewing our sense of place in the world."

John and Georgine McGowan

"Our lifestyle has changed."

In 1968, John McGowan, builder-designer, civil engineer, and licensed contractor, visited the pre-Columbian ruins at Mesa Verde, Colorado. As a builder, he was inspired by the structures, which reveal a highly developed understanding of passive solar heating by the Indians, and "became obsessed" with a dream to build a house using the same techniques. He studied up on how the Indians made use of adobe and stone in floors and walls to collect and store heat in winter; how the roofing with adobe and timbers of pine in the traditional *latilla* and *viga* forms added further insulation; and how their hunting groups dug their shelters into the ground to protect themselves against the winter winds, insulating the walls and roofs with adobe to absorb the sun's rays.

McGowan's updated version of an Indian "pit house" is set into a northwestern slope near Santa Fe, New Mexico. Adjustments to contemporary needs include skylights and windows ("we couldn't live with the darkness") and a small indoor pool. McGowan built the house with the help of his wife, Georgine, and paid relatives and friends, including several women, to help with the construction.

To the southeast of the house, McGowan built a separate solar structure, whose 10-foot-high water-type collectors are designed to supply the house with both heat and hot water. The adobe walls of the one-level, 1200-square-foot house are 4 to 5 feet thick and are covered on the outside with a waterproof plastic membrane and a layer of stucco cement. The foundation is rock with adobe flooring. Six inches below the flooring, McGowan installed copper pipes to conduct heat via hot water through the house. Their backup heat source, a kerosene-fired boiler, is used only during the winter months; they save around $80 a month over conventional heating systems.

The McGowan pit house, set almost totally below ground, is one example of a house design that causes the least disturbance to the natural environment. The entrance is practically the only hint of its existence. The structure, to the right of the photo, houses the McGowans' solar collectors.

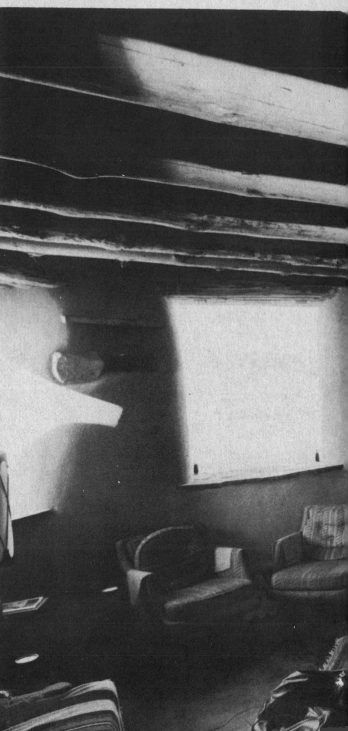

Georgine McGowan and friends enjoy the indoor communal bathing pool (left). Windows, skylights, the adobe fireplace and the huge beams that support the weight of the earthen walls and roof, contribute to the living room's ambiance (below). Once inside, one would hardly guess that the house is almost totally below ground.

The roof is constructed of exposed wood beams (the Spanish *latillas*), a layer of burlap covered by a sheet of waterproof plastic, and then 2 inches of Styrofoam insulation sandwiched between two layers of pumice cement. The final layer is a thin one of tar and gravel. "We tried," McGowan explained, "to keep the weight load as light as possible."

The materials for the pit house cost about $20 per square foot, or roughly $24,000; and $5,000 for the solar unit. If they had used skilled labor, McGowan estimates, the expense would have doubled, because of the detailed workmanship that only someone building his own structure could accomplish. John McGowan adds that the house could have been done for far less, as little as $15 a square foot, "but you have to be willing to go out and cut your own lumber and to spread the labor over a longer period."

The McGowans are happy with the way the house functions. "It has simplified our lives and helped us to attain peace and serenity," says John. Georgine concurs, adding that you don't need conventional furniture in a pit house. "Our lifestyle has changed," she says. "For example, one closet is enough for my clothes and one cupboard takes care of the dishes."

Stimulated by this experience, John McGowan has become a solar disciple. Predicting that "the day of the one-family house is on its way out," he now wants to build a pueblo-style community, "another Mesa Verde," geared to energy self-sufficiency—"without automobiles and without pollution."

Jim DeKorne

"If you want to change the world, change your own life."

Jim DeKorne, "fed up with high-tech city living," bought a 1-acre plot in the semi-arid hardscrabble region of northern New Mexico with a typical 1880s Spanish-style farmhouse on it. "I wanted to see if it was possible to live a Thoreau-like life with a wife and two kids," he says. At that time, a lot of people were talking about alternate-energy lifestyles, but few were actually doing anything about it. His goal was an "ecosystem" centered on a "survival greenhouse" that was powered by the wind, heated by the sun, and fed by compost.

Five years and a backbreaking effort later, Jim and his wife, Elizabeth, have an impressive achievement. Their greenhouse extends the growing season from ninety days to eight months without the aid of artificial light. The 12-volt, 200-watt wind generator supplies their essential electricity (although it turned out that the average wind speed was agonizingly just short of the 10 miles per hour needed for top efficiency). There is a root cellar, a work shed, chicken house, pigpen, and a bathhouse with a sauna. The DeKornes proved that an acre of near-desert could support four people without violating sound ecology—"not by repudiating technology but by enlightened use of it," Jim says.

At an elevation of about 7,000 feet, where the mean temperature is 47 degrees (only during June, July, and August does it rise above 60 degrees), the DeKornes' homestead at El Rito, New Mexico, has a short growing season and scarce water. So, they sunk the pit greenhouse, or "grow hole," 4 feet below ground. It is lined with cement blocks and covered over with fiberglass greenhouse sheets, using the earth for natural insulation. In winter the 1,400-gallon solar fish tank in the greenhouse supplies the heat for

At far left, Jim DeKorne adjusts the wind generator that supplies the power for his totally self-sufficient farmstead. The controls and batteries for the family's electricity are housed in the handmade log cabin nearby.

The "grow hole" supplies all of the DeKornes' food and vegetable staples. This semi-underground greenhouse is seen from the outside (left) and the inside (below). Here, DeKorne carries on his hydroponic gardening. Beneath the garden beds, he raises rabbits both for food and to provide fertilizer and carbon dioxide for the greenhouse.

growing vegetables. The wind generator supplies the power to circulate the tank water to a small flat plate solar collector and then through filters and back into the tank. The tank water is a "heat battery" storing solar energy during the day and radiating it back into the greenhouse at night.

After reading everything he could get from other ecology groups and from his own experiments, Jim found that hydroponics, gardening in a water rather than a soil medium, could triple the yield of conventional gardening. The vegetables are grown in 55-gallon drums cut in half the long way to make troughs filled with gravel. Two more drum halves are compost bins for earthworms that feed the fish in the aquaculture tank. Their casings are leached and go into the fertilizing soup for the plants. DeKorne also went back to the zodiacal calendar, not for astrological reasons but because the solstices and equinoxes provided reference points that fell in naturally with the yearly growing cycle.

The cycle of an ecosystem is continuous. For instance, rabbits, a buck, and three does live in cages on the greenhouse floor and supply an essential ingredient to the plants—carbon dioxide. That one element, Jim says, "can increase the vegetable yield from 15 to 70 percent." Rabbit droppings are used for fertilizer. And the rabbit meat is an excellent source of animal protein. "Four rabbits of good stock can yield about 400 pounds of protein in a year, or 100 pounds per person for a

The farmstead is studded with home-built outbuildings and animal pens. Below, Jim pats one of his pigs and, on the right, he stands in front of his workshop. This resourceful pioneer has written a book about his experiences in trying to live independent of corporate-controlled society.

family of four," he estimates. He feeds his animals commercial pellets, though, because the greenhouse produce couldn't feed both the family and the rabbits' numerous progeny.

Aquaculture, or fish farming, which seemed an attractive component of the ecosystem, turned out to be more difficult on trial. Stocking the tank was easy. The DeKornes drove to the nearest pond, 40 miles away, and caught bluegill sunfish on barbless hooks. But the fish required more energy to nurture than they gave back in food. At one point, the fish threatened to eat the whole earthworm population. Everything the DeKornes accomplished was the result of research, experiments, and frustrating trial and error.

Jim DeKorne has a masters degree in English and worked as a schoolteacher and also as a staff photographer for the Museum of New Mexico in Santa Fe. With no background in architecture, engineering, botany, or biology, he taught himself everything from scratch, including working with electricity. He also had no outside funding, and he believes this was an advantage. "I was forced to be creative and use ingenuity. I learned to plaster with adobe because I couldn't afford cement. There was no money to buy lumber, so I salvaged

it where I could. When I couldn't afford 50 cents for a metal screw, I had to make one myself." He feels "damned proud" of what he's done. "If someone cares enough they can do it without a grant," he adds.

In the near future, the DeKornes hope to build a 30-by-40-foot home with an attached greenhouse that would act as the solar collector to heat the house and would also provide much of the family's food. They plan to spend about $5,000, which is typical of the minimal budgeting all the way through their homesteading venture. The criterion for all their decisions is whether anybody could do what they did with very limited funds. In fact, their pioneering effort is outlined in a book that Jim DeKorne published and financed himself, a classic called *The Survival Greenhouse*.

"We did the book because we want to get other people started, so that they can learn from our mistakes as well as from our successes," says Jim, whose credo is Edmund Burke's dictum that "example is the school of mankind and they will learn at no other," adding, "If you want to change the world, change your own life."

Bill Yanda

This inexpensive greenhouse makes a pleasant and fruitful addition to the Yanda's house. Not only does it provide them with an abundance of vegetables throughout most of the year, but it also serves to heat a part of the main house and to provide play space for their child.

The "pit" house of John and Georgine McGowan in Santa Fe, New Mexico, (top, left) is mostly underground. The owner approaches the entrance. Only the steep roofs of the structure that holds the solar collectors protrude aboveground.

The residence of Steven and Sydell Lipson in a Connecticut suburb (left) was designed as a live-in greenhouse. The walls are made of air-filled plastic "pillows." These have proved as effective an insulation barrier as double-insulating glass at a fraction of the cost. Because the pillows are transparent the interior spaces (above) have an open, pavilion-like feeling.

The slanting wall rising out of the ground holds the solar collectors of Paul Davis's house in Corrales, New Mexico, (top) which he built himself. Neighbor Steve Baer's "zome" house can be seen in the background.

A crew of students and friends help to erect a Jacobs wind generator onto the tower of Kent Bloomer's windmill in Guilford, Connecticut (below). The first machine blew down in a violent windstorm.

Builder Michael Reynolds experimented with beer cans as the building material in his unusual habitation (above). The interior walls of the greenhouse (far left of photo) are constructed of water-filled beer cans, which act as solar heat collectors.

Hal Migel's house in Tesuque, New Mexico, has a greenhouse (below) that provides his family with a warm, indoor garden room in winter. In summer, the plastic sheeting of the greenhouse walls is removed and the space becomes an outdoor patio.

The round stucco drum of Migel's house (far right of photo, below) holds the living room. Running across the side of the house is the removeable greenhouse/patio.

The solar-heated adobe house that Karen Terry built for herself (above) rises in four broad steps of windows out of the Sante Fe, New Mexico, mountain terrain.

Developer Wayne Nichols calls his house a "solar hybrid" because it incorporates several ideas for utilizing the sun's energy: thick stucco walls for thermal mass, solar collectors for space and water heating, plus a greenhouse to extend the growing season into winter.

The unconventional design of solar engineer Everett Barber's house in Connecticut (below) derives from its energy-conserving features. The placement of windows, roof slope, dormers, and exterior surface all perform a function to aid solar heat gain and heat retention in winter and natural air cooling in summer.

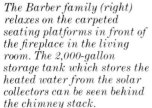

The Barber family (right) relaxes on the carpeted seating platforms in front of the fireplace in the living room. The 2,000-gallon storage tank which stores the heated water from the solar collectors can be seen behind the chimney stack.

This unusual house (above) was constructed out of prefabricated silos. Each of the three drums holds a living zone: one is for the living area, another for the bedroom, the third is a study-library. The solar collectors span the three roofs. The house is owned by Mr. and Mrs. Charles Swift and is situated in Lambertville, New Jersey.

Daniel Newman copied the design of the traditional Navaho hogan in this house he built in Cerrillos, New Mexico, for his family. The skylight at the top is a refinement that brings light into the large one-room interior.

Architect David Wright's house (right) is an adobe building which is heated passively by the sun. In front of it, however, is a small solar collector that provides the hot water supply for the house.

Inside, (above) Wright's long window seat has water-filled drums buried underneath it. These soak in the sun all day and radiate their stored heat back into the interiors at night.

The contemporary design of Douglas Kelbaugh's solar-heated house in Princeton, New Jersey, (opposite page bottom) fits in nicely with its traditionally styled neighbors. The screened extension is a greenhouse.

The "zomes" of solar pioneer Steve Baer's house shine like a metallic spacecraft on the New Mexico landscape. The windmill pumps the water for the Baer household and also for those of two neighbors.

Denver architect Richard Crowther designed this year-round residence with the solar collectors mounted both vertically, as part of the southern facade, and at an angle, horizontally, as part of the roof.

Professor Richard Davis braved the cloudy east coast climate to build this solar house in Bar Harbor, Maine. The solar collectors occupy two-thirds of the southern facade of the house. They adjoin a greenhouse and a deck.

The living area of the Davis house is a combination kitchen, dining, and living room so that the space shares heat from three sources: sun-warmed greenhouse air when that door is left opened, cooking heat, and a wood-burning fireplace (not shown).

"Technology cannot cure our ills. You have to have faith in the people to do it."

Bill Yanda spends much of his time traveling around the Southwest demonstrating the concept of "heat-and-eat" housing to low-income groups. He has already built eleven of the experimental lean-to greenhouses—such as the one he and his wife, Susan, have in Nambe, New Mexico—in villages in the northern part of the state. The heat-and-eat idea, which is a fast-growing wrinkle on the natural-energy scene, is hardly new. In the 1800s, Yankee farmers used the lean-to greenhouse as a source for extra food and warmth.

The Yandas have given the greenhouse new prominence by their enthusiasm. "We took it to the people, to the dirt farmers, to people on fixed and low incomes, 70 percent of them Chicanos or Indians. We showed them it could be done at very low materials costs, $1.85 per square foot in 1975." The price of materials may change, but their design is amazingly inexpensive if the owner uses indigenous materials such as second-hand lumber for the structure or homemade adobe brick.

The Yandas got their idea for the greenhouse while gardening some time back. "We kept records of seed germination, plant growth, and temperatures and discovered that heat buildup inside the greenhouse is tremendous even in winter—it can register 115 degrees at the apex. So it occurred to us to attach the greenhouse to the house, letting the hot air convect naturally through the connecting windows and doors," Bill Yanda said. With simple construction methods and materials, a greenhouse goes up in a hurry. A greenhouse with a surface of 300 square feet can be installed within two to three hours. A double layer of translucent sheeting laid over a wood frame sandwiches air between fiberglass sheets on the outside and soft polyethylene sheets on the inside.

The Yandas (Bill is an ex-bluegrass musician who is working toward a master's degree from Antioch College on the study of self-help natural-energy uses) are put off by the exotic applications of solar technology on houses. They are seriously looking for alternatives—basic survival principles that everyone, especially the poor, can afford. The couple are directors of the Solar Sustenance Project, a nonprofit research and educational group that they founded with a grant from the Four Corners Regional Commission of New Mexico. Susan is secretary of the New Mexico Solar Energy Association.

Depending on its length and how it ties onto the house, the greenhouse, they found, can provide a home with 80 percent of its total winter heating needs. By their estimate, 1 square foot of south-facing greenhouse wall picks up enough solar heat for 2 square feet of the house, or twice the area it occupies. By prolonging the growing season, the produce raised in the greenhouse can become an important food supplement while lowering the grocery bills.

The Yandas maintain that their concept could turn into a nationwide boon for saving fossil fuel. From November until mid-July, most of the country has to rely on produce shipped from distant points. That processing and transport are a huge energy drain. "Best of all," say the Yandas, "this low-tech, low-key solution places a minimal financial and maintenance burden on the family. There's not much to do but water the plants and control the insects." It all ties in with Bill's populist view: "Technology cannot cure our ills," he says. "You have to have faith in the people to do it."

Steven Lipson

"There is a certain joy living in a cool environment. We live beneath an umbrella of nature—oaks, birches, maples."

Sydell and Steven Lipson (who was working in his father's florist shop in New Haven, Connecticut) wanted to build a "live-in" greenhouse—one large, plant-filled space that would get most of its heating from the sun. They had seen the experimental house with transparent plastic walls that architect Mark Hildebrand had built for himself in the woods, and they asked him for a refined version that could be bank-financed. The Lipsons' 4-acre plot is next to a forest preserve in the conservative township of Hamden, Connecticut. Their "street-conscious" neighbors "didn't want a bomb on the street," says architect Hildebrand, so the design of the house had to be appropriate to the community.

His design for the Lipsons' house appears to run counter to energy-saving theories because three walls of the house are transparent. They are made of two sheets of hermetically sealed polyvinyl chloride (PVC) plastic with an air space in between. Hildebrand had first seen the "pillow" walls used in Colorado and had tried it out on his own house before adapting the technique for the Lipsons' house. "I was experimenting with industrial materials to replace timber construction and thought of plastic because it was economical," he explains. The PVC he chose had good standards for longevity and visual clarity. But the material, used commercially for packing and wrapping, is thought of as disposable and, if subjected to stress, can become brittle and crack.

"We had to design the pillows and install them so that in erection or inflation, they would never be taxed," says Hildebrand. When inflated, the skin stiffens and the plastic forms both the interior and exterior surfaces. The pillows are clamped in place with extruded aluminum frames, similar to the ones that hold storefront windows.

Hildebrand experimented with several different methods of sealing the plastic sheets together, sealing them with heat, by working with the kind of zippers used for underwater camera bags, and by radio frequency. He ended up using radio frequency and got a local factory to seal the plastic sheets into pillow forms. "I did some con-

Shaded in woodland, the Lipson house in Hamden, Connecticut, has three walls made up of air-filled plastic "pillows." The roof line slopes from a two-story height on the south to an eight-foot low on the north. Inside, the double-height space is enough room for the sleeping loft, above, which is the platform over the entry door.

Despite the double thickness of the air-filled pillows, they are surprisingly transparent and give the living area a greenhouse feeling. This insulating barrier is about as effective as Thermopane glass, the Lipsons say. Only in the dead of winter do they have to rely on their pot-bellied stove and their electric heaters for additional heat.

sulting work for them in exchange for using their sealing equipment," he says. The advantage of the plastic pillows, according to Hildebrand, is that they insulate as well as Thermopane glass—at about one-tenth the cost. However, because of the impermanence of plastic, the pillows will probably have to be replaced every three to five years, adding to maintenance costs.

Since so much of the house is transparent, its siting and profile had to be carefully planned. The roof is angled upward toward the south, creating a two-story living room with maximum exposure to the sun, while the north profile is low, heavily insulated, and windowless except for a back door. A roof overhang juts out enough to shield the pillow walls in summer but allows the sun to penetrate all the way to the north wall in winter. The living area is essentially one space for living and dining with a separate sleeping loft. The kitchen and bath are tucked under the low north side.

Rather than clear the site, the Lipsons kept as many trees as possible for natural climate control. In summer, the leafy trees shade the house, while in winter their bare limbs let the sun through. "Without ventilation," says Sydell Lipson, "the interiors can get up to 120 degrees." The house is designed for natural gravitation of air through vents—placed low on the north side and high on the south—that set up a strong air current through the interiors. "In the winter, we open the vents for two or three hours during the day and close them around the middle of the afternoon, when it's about 85 degrees, to conserve heat for the evening," she explains. On cold nights they start a fire in their Franklin stove, consuming about 3 cords of wood for the heating season.

Connecticut building codes stipulate that all four walls of a dwelling must be able to be heated to an average 68 degrees, which necessitated an auxiliary heat source. The Lipsons and architect Hildebrand weighed the advantages of units that were expensive to use but cheaper to purchase against expensive units that were cheap to operate—and chose a type of electric heater commonly used in theater lobbies. It is relatively inex-

pensive but eats up a lot of electricity. They also installed an infrared heater for the bathroom because it is the most efficient means to warm up surface temperatures. "The minute you turn it on and stand under it the skin of the body is warmed," says Hildebrand. "Other units have to heat the air first before the air heats the body."

Concessions must be made to living in a house with no central heating system, say the Lipsons. "Most people find our house chilly in winter," says Sydell, "but you learn to live and dress differently. In the daytime, you can go naked in the house, but at night you may have to put on three sweaters. When friends come over in winter, I arm them with sweaters when they walk through the door." The Lipsons also tend to use the house in zones. Some areas are warm, and others are allowed to become quite cool. The area within 12 feet of the wood-burning stove (which is set on tiles to absorb and radiate the heat) and the kitchen, which receives warmth from cooking, are used intensively. "We get as close to the wood-burning stove, a nice warm object, as we can," Sydell says. "Some days, I feel like a big squaw, cooking up a storm to heat up the entire house. We've also taken to sitting up on the loft, where it's warmer."

The Lipsons rely on their electric heaters only in the dead of winter. "If we go to a movie and won't be building a fire in the stove, we put them on for a couple of hours. Once or twice last winter when it dropped below zero and we were afraid that the pipes might freeze, we put the heaters on from three to five A.M.," Sydell said. And yet the Lipsons' electricity bills are low, running an average of about $35 per month in winter and $40 for the coldest month, January.

The 36-by-32-foot house cost the couple $30,000 to build, but they economized by doing most of the work themselves. They had no building experience, nor were they even particularly handy, and it took them five months to build the house. "Sydell worked on the house with me and Bill Duesing, an associate, every day, and Steve helped out on weekends," Mark Hildebrand reports.

"They learned many skills and made contributions at each stage of building. By the end, they were very comfortable in their own ability to control and modify their living environment." Hildebrand estimates that their contribution saved thousands of dollars and permitted them such luxuries as hand-sanded and -oiled exposed wood beams and columns throughout the house.

Because the house was experimental in many ways, there are things about it that the Lipsons would now change. "We should have designed it with a way to store that 120-degree heat from the daytime to carry over into the night. Because the house is so handsome now, it is a problem to integrate a heat storage system into the existing design," Sydell says. Window shades or curtains could solve part of that problem, and they are investigating various materials; at present, white window-shade material appears to offer the best in terms of economy and efficiency. The plastic "pillow" walls have held up extremely well, in their opinion. "The house suits our lifestyle," Mrs. Lipson says. "We like living in the woods. There is a certain joy in living in a cool environment. We live beneath an umbrella of nature—oaks, birches, maples. In summer, the forest floor is very cool. I now find I don't function very well in a house with central heating; it dulls me and makes me sleepy. And my husband gets a lot of exercise chopping wood. If he comes home feeling frustrated, he takes it out on chopping a cord of wood."

Lee Porter Butler

"You can design any building in any climate to maintain any temperature you want simply by balancing the relationship of mass, insulation, and orientation."

The house that Lee Porter Butler built for his family on a 200-acre site in the densely wooded West Tennessee hills is something of a fantasy: it has twenty-six rooms on four levels, with indoor gardens and swimming pool, ponds of tropical fish, and two waterfalls. Luxury aside, the house (which cost him approximately $150,000 to build in 1972) exemplifies ecological construction and design.

Butler, who was a builder for ten years before becoming an architect and who has since relocated to San Francisco, made the house an experiment. He was then formulating the environmental design theories that have since become the spearhead of his career. At first he planned to heat the house with water-type flat plate solar collectors, until he found that the collectors would cost $10,000 for a house of its size, measuring 70 feet square and 40 feet high. "I worked out a more passive solution based on an integrated energy environment," he says. That passive solution revolves around the house's soaring greenhouse, which faces south and takes up nearly

The Butler-designed house in Tennessee looks large and indeed it is. It includes about 26 rooms on four levels. The large indoor greenhouse takes up about half of the space. Butler (above) has since relocated to San Francisco where he specializes in designing energy-conscious buildings.

Butler designed the house for interior climate control by natural means through cold and hot seasons. The greenhouse area covers nearly the same floor space as the house's living quarters and there are complex provisions for air circulation. Vents and dampers direct solar heated air into the rooms to warm them or force summer heat out through the top of the house to cool it. The angle of the balcony is calculated so that the summer sun misses the house interiors. The bed of earth and rock beneath the house, as well as a water pool, act as reservoirs to provide heat in winter and cool air in summer. In addition, intake vents in the earth bring air through ducts into the house, routing it through the interiors for summer air cooling.

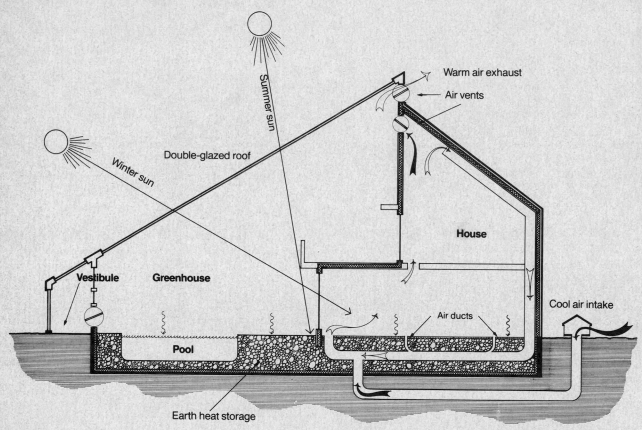

Summer sun

Winter sun

Double-glazed roof

Warm air exhaust

Air vents

House

Vestibule   Greenhouse

Cool air intake

Air ducts

Pool

Earth heat storage

half of the indoor living space.

The greenhouse acts as the solar heat collector, building up the sun-heated air. The air circulates by natural convection through tubes down to an insulated earth bed, where it is stored and can be retrieved when needed (see diagram).

"Only a very small amount of heat is lost through walls and ceiling," Butler contends. "Most of the heat is lost through cracks, doors, and other openings, where cold air enters and must be

heated, then moves out of the house and is replaced by more cold air." Because of the greenhouse's double glazing and its high temperatures (60 to 70 percent higher than outdoors), it acts as a buffer and minimizes heat loss. With most windows facing south and virtually no east-, west-, or north-facing windows, plus vestibules at the entry doors, the intake of cold outside air is further reduced.

The house is also designed so that natural air

currents ventilate it in summer. Cool air that enters from the underground tubes and the intake valve outside the house (see diagram) pushes the hot air out through the high point of the building. This natural air conditioning is distributed to each room through ducts and cuts the cooling load to one-third that of a conventional house in the same locale, Butler estimates.

Six months after the family moved into the house a severe ice storm with zero temperatures hit the region and Butler found his backup propane gas tank empty, "because I couldn't afford to refill it," he recalls. To his amazement, the inside temperature of the house stayed at a steady 68 degrees except for one night when it dropped to 58 degrees. (Now he speculates that double glazing on the north window would have reduced even that heat loss.) After the experience with the storm, Butler kept wondering why the house remained so warm. "One day I went out in the woods and lay down under a pine tree, watching it sway in the wind, and the answer came to me in a flash: You can design any building in any climate to maintain any temperature you want, simply by balancing the relationship between mass, insulation, and orientation," he says. "The basic equation is simple: mass equals the sum of all the heat transfers divided by the change in temperature of the mass. If you want to live in a house where the temperature never varies by more than ten degrees, design it so that ten times the mass is equal to all the energy flowing out."

Butler developed this thesis into what he calls "natural-energy architecture." Most houses, if properly oriented to the sun, can provide that necessary mass through their own building materials. Philosophically, it means to be in balance with the natural environment. "We can live quite well without our highly sophisticated machinery," he claims. "Our reliance on high technology is the chief cause of our present environmental crisis. If we admit that, then all kinds of possibilities open up to improve the quality of our lives."

The interior of the greenhouse resembles a large, plant-filled atrium. A bridge in the center leads over a pool, providing access to the main part of the house.

Richard Crowther

"It's immoral to burn coal and gas to heat and cool a house."

Perhaps it was the effect of growing up in the Depression years or perhaps it was the dictate of a frugal nature that led architect Richard Crowther into energy-conscious design. Whatever the motivation, his commitment underlies his architectural practice in Denver. In fact, few architects have been able to complete as many solar buildings, fifteen to date, ranging from single-family dwellings and vacation houses to plans for office buildings and condominiums. Crowther's buildings are remarkably individual. No two houses or buildings look alike, although each draws its design direction from the climate, location, and from a long list of energy-saving features, which he and his staff have formulated.

Although most of the buildings and houses have been completed since 1972, Crowther's interest in solar-energy design dates much farther back. Early in his forty-year career, which includes graphic, interior, and restaurant design as well as industrial design and architecture, Crowther was intrigued by the effect of climate on buildings. "I have been thinking about energy conservation since 1929," he says, "and the concept of solar energy was always important to me." Twenty-four

From the outside, the Crowther house in a Denver suburb appears to be quite fortress-like. But inside (below), the skylight brings in enough sunshine for a garden of plants to flourish next to the dining room. Architect Richard Crowther stands in the foreground.

Crowther designed his own house based on passive solar build-ing principles. In it he incorporated many of the energy-sav-ing features which his office makes its specialty: the materials and color were selected for their ability to absorb heat; the building is thickly insulated, and doors and windows are recessed to protect them from wind buffetting. The roof is pur-posely flat to allow the build-up of a blanket of snow as addi-tional wintertime insulation.

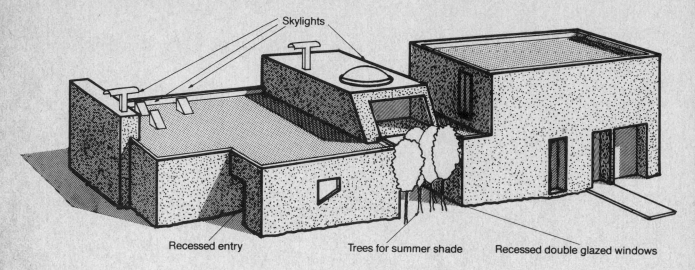

Skylights

Recessed entry   Trees for summer shade   Recessed double glazed windows

years ago, Crowther designed a house with south-facing windows to collect the sun's heat during the day and with thick thermal walls to retain it over-night. "I wasn't thinking of solar energy per se," he says. "I just did it because it seemed like the sensible thing to do."

Today, his firm, Crowther/Solar Group, incorpo-rates a list of almost one hundred energy-saving features into every house and building that it designs. The list covers advantageous siting and beneficial landscaping; the use of overhangs, ves-tibules, recessed windows, heavy insulation; plac-ing certain rooms and the garage as wind buffers; using durable, low-maintenance materials in con-struction; sinking the house partly below grade and giving it a low-profile to the north; plus designing it for cooling by natural air convection and recycling heat from appliances back into the house in winter.

Although many of the houses Crowther designs today incorporate solar collectors, his own house, built in 1972, is a totally passive solar building. It is situated on a suburban street in a residential section of Denver. The 2,600-square-foot building has an attached 1,200-square-foot rental apart-ment. Crowther designed the building shell to be a solar collector in winter and to reject the sun's heat in summer. The skin of the building is com-posed of wood framing of two-by-six posts fin-ished on the inside with dry wall and the recesses filled with fiberglass insulation. The exterior is surfaced in a metal lath and then stuccoed. The flat roof is similarly constructed and topped with a layer of light-colored gravel.

The placement of the windows is carefully planned to protect them from buffeting by wind. Most of them are deeply recessed, some as much as 6 feet, from the exterior building plane. Sky-lights are also carefully placed to bring in both light and heat, oriented toward the sun's angle in winter in order to bring in five to six hours of sunlight on even the shortest days.

The floors beneath the windows and skylights serve as thermal reservoirs, according to Crowther. They are made up of 4-inch-thick con-crete on insulated slab, which is placed over a

The interiors of solar heated houses are often quite surprisingly spartan. The rooms in this Crowther-designed house, owned by Murray and Diane Watts, is casually furnished, full of light, and open in feeling. The fireplace and exposed wood beams lend an old-fashioned touch to an otherwise contemporary room. A poster inviting friends and neighbors to their solar house-warming party hangs on the living room wall.

gravel base. In all, the layers create a 3-foot-thick thermal mass.

In Denver's snowy climate, the use of a flat roof rather than a snow-dispelling pitched roof was also calculated. Crowther favors the buildup of snow in winter as an additional insulation blanket. In summer, the light-colored gravel covering the roof deflects the sun's rays. The house exterior of acrylic stucco is painted a gray, veering toward the dark end of the spectrum, to be heat absorbing because of the house's location in a northern climate.

A bonus of the skylighted interiors is the indoor garden atmosphere. Crowther keeps tree-sized plants beneath the lights, not only for their attractiveness but also to help freshen the air, since plants absorb carbon dioxide. A water fountain provides humidification of the interior air in winter, and also serves to raise the perceived temperature. To cool the house in summer, air is circulated through a vent system by natural convection and augmented when necessary by fans. The house is also equipped with a 4-ton central air conditioner.

Crowther designed the 2,000 square foot residence (above) as a prototype for use as a solar-heated single city family dwelling, or for cluster housing. The 28-foot-square building has bedrooms at ground level; living, dining rooms and kitchen on the main level, and a studio on the third level. The water-type solar collectors are roof-mounted at a 53 degree angle. There is also a small greenhouse at ground level. On another house (right), designed for the Murray Watts, the collectors are integrated both on the sloping roof and, vertically, on the south-facing side walls.

In an unusually rigorous year, the total fuel bill for heating and cooling the house was as low as $102. Of that figure, Crowther estimates that $30 was spent to run the air conditioner and the remaining $72 was for fuel oil. In winter the Crowthers keep the thermostat set at 70 to 72 degrees. The house is equipped with a forced-air oil furnace for supplementary heat. The passive systems and energy-optimized features of the house provide 65 percent of the heating and 60 percent of the cooling.

Four other houses designed by Crowther/Solar Group all utilize flat plate collectors. In an early experiment, Crowther bought a small older house with the notion of refitting it for solar heating. In the process, the house was completely redesigned for both aesthetic and energy-saving features. The roof was tilted at a 53-degree angle to accommodate an air-type collector. Adjoining this house, Crowther designed a new house, a 28-by-28-foot square building, intended as a prototype for a small single-family residence, or adaptable to cluster and townhouse plans. The new house was fitted with a water-type solar collection system.

Crowther intended to compare the two types to see which was more economical, easier to install, and more efficient in operation. Although the tests were not conclusive in every detail, Crowther now favors the air-to-rock system and has used it exclusively on his later buildings.

The main problem with the water-type system, which pumps water from the 570-square-foot collectors on the roof to a 1,000-gallon water tank, was that the pumps burned out. The water collectors themselves also proved to be slightly more expensive per square foot than the air types. But he found the system to be very efficient, supplying 90 percent of the space heating and 100 percent of the hot water supply.

The houses were intended as income-producing properties, and the converted house was rented to a young bachelor, while the new house was rented to a working couple. (Both tenants, it turns out, drive small, economical European cars.) His ten-ants enjoy living in solar-heated houses, and have no complaints about either heat or hot water, the landlord claims.

The house designed for Murray and Diane Watts is yet another illustration of the remarkable variety in solar house design. It is a year-round residence for a family of four, situated in a pine forest clearing northwest of Golden, Colorado. The solar collectors are mounted in two positions, angled at the roofline and vertical along the front facade. The 370 square feet of air-type collectors store their heat in a heat storage bin containing 7 tons of gravel. The solar system supplies 80 percent of the space heating for the four-bedroom house as well as the building's hot water supply.

Terracor, a Salt Lake City-based developer, has another Crowther-designed house, a prototype for a planned community in Golden, Colorado. The asking price of the house is $115,000, and John Kurowski, the general manager of Terracor, esti-

The diagram for the four-bedroom house on the preceding pages illustrates the use of recessed windows and balconies to shield them from the wind. The 370 square feet of collectors provide the building with most of the space heating as well as the hot water supply. For additional protection from winter winds the garage is strategically placed at the east end of the house and the building is banked with earth berms on both the north and west sides.

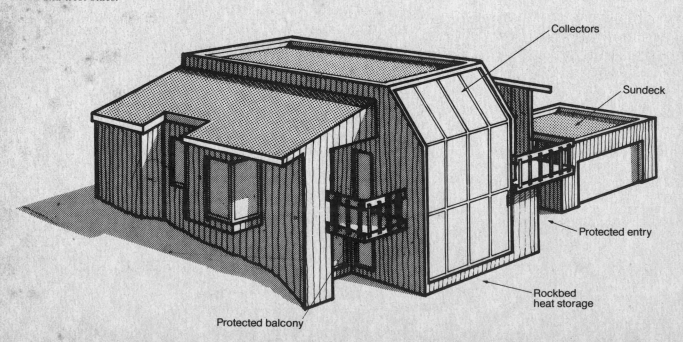

Collectors

Sundeck

Protected entry

Rockbed heat storage

Protected balcony

mates that the solar-energy system accounts for $10,000 of that figure. The three-level, 3,800-square-foot residence is an exceedingly handsome design, and the solar collectors are set unobtrusively into the roof. The solar heating system is an air-type collector, storing the heat in a rock bin located on the lower level. The system supplies 80 percent of the space heating.

Kurowski claims that public reaction to the solar-heated house has been "outstanding." Terracor's exhibit at a local home show attracted inquiries from over four hundred people, all of whom requested an invitation to tour the house on its official opening.

Energy savings are difficult to assess for the Crowther properties because of a highly controversial rate structure set by Denver's gas utility company. The less natural gas that is used in this region, the more it costs. One house Crowther remodeled was equipped with a gas heating system. With the installation of extra insulation and other energy-conscious features, its gas consumption dropped from a yearly average of 1,217 cubic feet to a consumption of 11.6 cubic feet, or an astronomical drop of 99 percent. Because of the extremely high rates for first-end use, however, the utility bill dropped only a few dollars from $103 to $89.

Crowther's group is presently fighting for a change in the rate structure for natural gas in the Denver area. They believe that it penalizes small energy users and encourages the use of more expensive energy. Time will tell how successful their fight on this issue will be. Inequitable rate structures are not confined to Denver, and winning this battle may set a precedent for a nationwide change.

This house is a prototype for a planned solar-heated community near Golden, Colorado. The roof-mounted collectors are integrated neatly into the building's overall design. Here Crowther effectively demonstrates how development housing can be aesthetically-satisfying and fuel-saving as well.

Richard Davis

"You live differently in a solar house. We are much more aware of what the weather is doing."

In its first year of operation, Norah and Richard Davis's solar house attracted two thousand tourists. "We finally had to put up a 'No Trespassing' sign," Richard Davis said. A transplanted southerner who went north to Bar Harbor, Maine, to teach philosophy at The College of the Atlantic, Professor Davis wanted to build a house out of recycled materials. On the advice of a colleague at the college, architect Ernest McMullen, his plans were expanded to include a solar heating system and a wind generator.

Locating recycled materials wasn't that easy, although the Davises did discover some interesting "finds": the ballroom floor, doors, and 12-foot-long counters are from the Evelyn Walsh McLean mansion (she was famous for owning the Hope Diamond, now in the Smithsonian Institution); structural timbers from a razed sardine factory; and a 2,000-gallon gasoline tank from a filling station to store their solar-heated water. "We didn't save much money using recycled materials," Richard says, "but we got materials we couldn't otherwise afford—the 1½-inch solid wood doors and the quarter-sawn oak floors, for instance."

The Davis house is a compact, 1,300-square-foot building with an open interior plan for the living-dining-kitchen area, two bedrooms, and a utility room. Expenses came to about $30,000.

The solar collectors, a trim bank of 26-foot-long fiberglass-faced panels, take up about half of the southern facade of the house; a greenhouse that opens to the kitchen and a deck occupies the rest of the front. Despite its conservative design, the Davises had difficulty obtaining a mortgage for a solar-heated house. "The local banks turned us down because they felt the house was too risky," architect McMullen recalls. "Finally, I wrote a letter to John Cole, editor of *The Maine Times*, an

This compact solar-heated house in Maine, the home of a professor at The College of the Atlantic in Bar Harbor, sits on a rocky ledge. The location of the house was dictated by the desire of Richard Davis to have a wind generator, but the coastal winds proved to be too gusty for the system and it had to be abandoned. The living room (above right) adjoins a small greenhouse (right) where the family cat is happiest.

environmental tabloid, who wrote to one of the trustees of the Depositor's Trust up here and *shamed* the bank into granting the construction loan." Even then, it took a two-and-a-half-month effort, during which time the bank hired outside consultants and architects who flew up in chartered planes from Portland at the Davises' expense. "And they knew nothing about solar heating systems," says McMullen.

The house conforms to McMullen's—and a grow- ing number of other architects'—concept of energy-saving design: that the right combination of materials for thermal mass, siting, and fenestration will keep a house significantly warmer in winter regardless of climate, without having to install expensive solar hardware. A design change advocated by engineers and architects concerned about fuel waste is incorporated in the Davis house: instead of conventional two-by-fours, the building is framed with two-by-eight studs to

The Davis house is simple and straightforward in plan (below). The solar water-type collectors take up about half of the southern facade, sharing space with the greenhouse and the sun deck. The solar heated water storage bin lies below the collectors. It consists of a recycled 2,000-gallon gasoline tank embedded in crushed rock. Crawl space under most of the house serves as a plenum for distribution of warm air to the rooms. The hot water tank for the house's water supply resides inside the main tank and is heated by it. Owner Richard Davis and architect Ernest McMullen stand in the living room (right).

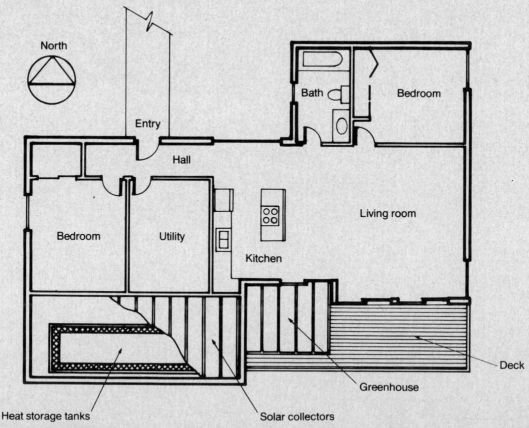

North

Entry

Hall

Bath

Bedroom

Bedroom

Utility

Kitchen

Living room

Heat storage tanks

Solar collectors

Greenhouse

Deck

118

make a deeper recess for wall insulation. The house is insulated with 7 inches of fiberglass batts in the walls and 9½ inches in the ceiling.

McMullen's solar design combines features of the basic water, air-to-rock, and greenhouse solar heat systems. The roof-mounted collector is composed of corrugated aluminum sheeting under fiberglass. Water is piped up to a feeder pipe at the top of the corrugated sheeting, where it trickles down the gullies and is heated by the sun to 120 degrees. The water collects in a trough at the bottom of the collector, and from there it flows down into a 2,000-gallon water storage tank that is embedded in a rock bin below the house. Beneath the rock bin is a manifold constructed out of standard concrete block. Air is circulated through the manifold, picking up heat from the rock bin, and then distributed through ducts to the rooms. The Davises' hot water supply is also tied into the solar system.

The architect and his clients, who liked this par-

ticular solar system because it was simple and inexpensive, bought the basic plans from solar engineer Harry Thomason of Washington, D.C. It cost about $1,500 to build and install. "It isn't the most efficient for heat transfer, but you can afford to have a larger collector area because it is cheaper," Davis explains. "If we had bought a General Electric unit of 20 square feet of prefabricated collectors, we wouldn't stand a chance to recoup our investment," he adds. He also used Kalwall fiberglass instead of glass to cover the collectors, because "you can nail it on in sheets." During the shakedown phase, the plastic feeder pipe they used in the collector melted into a "blob of spaghetti" and had to be replaced with copper. The Davises also found that a larger-capacity storage tank would have given the house more heat. Their 2,000-gallon tank was supposed to store enough heat for three successive cloudy days—but they forgot to take into account Maine's strong coastal winds.

"If we have sunny winter days that aren't too
windy, with temperatures around 30 degrees, we
can just get by on the solar heating system. If it
starts to go below 30 degrees and the wind picks
up, we have to resort to our wood-burning furnace," Davis explains. But their auxiliary heat
source is work to keep going. "It isn't the ideal
solution," Davis admits. "You have to stoke it
twice a day and have a friend come by to check it
if you go away." The first winter of its use, the
furnace consumed about 5½ cords of wood. Some
days, however, the temperature in the greenhouse
can rise to 100 degrees, and then the main room
tends to overheat, at which point the Davises end
up having to open windows. (They do enjoy their
fresh lettuce and nearly year-round tomato crop,
however.)

The wind generating system did not fare well
for the Davises. Strong winds damaged two windmills in succession, so Davis gave up and donated
them to the college for research. "I would still love
to build one that would work," he muses. He tried
to get a research grant for the wind system, and
even though he knows Senator Muskie and has
other government friends, "the grants always go
to major corporations." Because the original plans
included a wind generator on the site, the house
was built on a bluff and it should have been better
protected from the prevailing winds. "In a dead
calm, the solar system operates very well to heat
the house, but that rarely obtains," Davis says.
"More often we have winds of 25 to 30 miles per
hour, and that uses up heat fast.

"We have adjusted to the fact that a solar house
isn't capable of responding rapidly to changes in
temperature," he adds. "For instance, if we come
home at night and the inside temperature has
dropped to the mid-50s, it takes a while for the
stored heat to warm the house up to the 60s. In
early winter, we keep the house at 70 degrees, but
as it gets colder, we feel comfortable at 65
degrees. You live differently in a solar house," he
says. "We are much more aware of what the
weather is doing."

Douglas Kelbaugh

"It's not very difficult to design a solar house."

Architect Douglas Kelbaugh, who works for the city of Trenton, New Jersey, read an article in a British architectural magazine about the Trombe-Michel house in southern France. That house is famous for the "Trombe" wall, a massive masonry wall, facing south, used to absorb the sun's heat. "I fell in love with the idea," Kelbaugh remembers. "Especially since my wife and I had been living in an old stone farmhouse near Lambertville, New Jersey, and its 18-inch-thick walls worked along the same lines." He also liked the design potential the concept offered. "Even if it turned out not to be the most efficient heating system, I liked the aesthetic possibilities; the simplicity appealed to me."

Kelbaugh adapted the idea to his site, a 60-by-100-foot plot in Princeton, New Jersey, and to the urban conditions, an area with a net density of seven units per acre. He designed a two-story house with an attached greenhouse, "more or less intuitively," with builder Nate Bard of Roosevelt, New Jersey. They used locally available and relatively cheap materials, such as glass, wood, and concrete.

Kelbaugh describes his Trombe-inspired solar design as follows: Collection of the sun's energy is

Douglas Kelbaugh's glass-faced house stands out in marked contrast to its suburban-style neighbors on a Princeton, N.J., street. Despite the emphatic architectural statement it makes on the outside, the interiors (below) are warm and inviting.

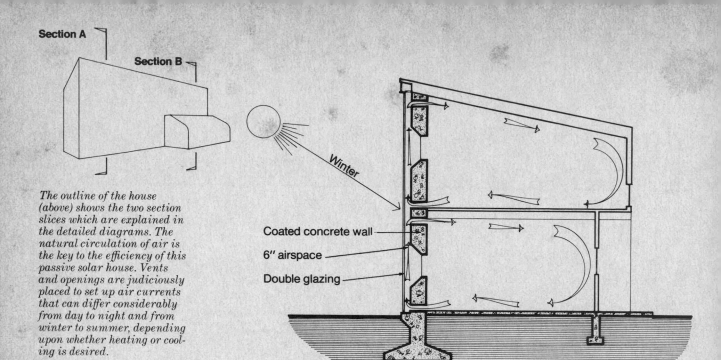

Section A
Section B

The outline of the house (above) shows the two section slices which are explained in the detailed diagrams. The natural circulation of air is the key to the efficiency of this passive solar house. Vents and openings are judiciously placed to set up air currents that can differ considerably from day to night and from winter to summer, depending upon whether heating or cooling is desired.

Coated concrete wall

6" airspace

Double glazing

Winter

Section A Winter day

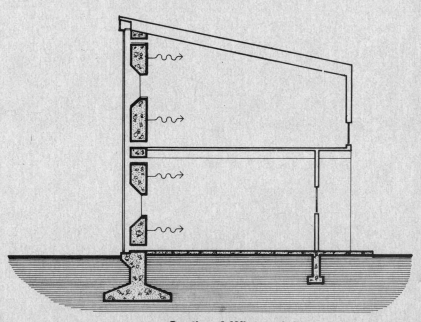

The sketches (right), illustrate the air flow during winter. At top, the sun strikes the glass window, which has a thick, masonry wall directly behind it, warming up both the wall and the air in the space between. Air flows into the cavity in front of the wall, is heated by the sun and passes through an opening at the top of the Trombe wall into the rooms. Here it forms a wide circular pattern and moves back to the Trombe wall. On a winter night, the building is heated primarily by the sun's heat stored in the thick masonry wall.

Section A Winter night

Even more sun-heated air is generated in the large greenhouse space adjacent to the main area. The greenhouse floor is a thick masonry slab and it, too, absorbs heat as the sun pounds down upon it, and then reradiates the warmth back into the room.

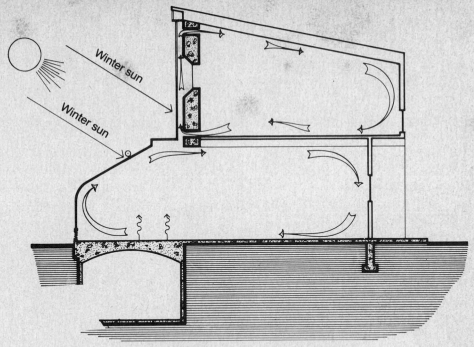

Section B Winter day at greenhouse

In the evening, a screen is rolled down over the glass to retard loss of heat. The thick masonry greenhouse floor is also sending back into the interiors all of the sun's heat absorbed by day.

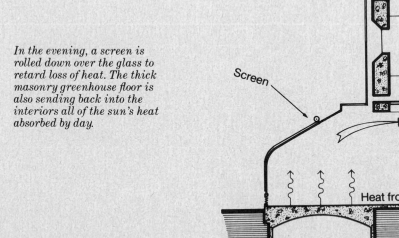

Screen

Heat from slab & cellar

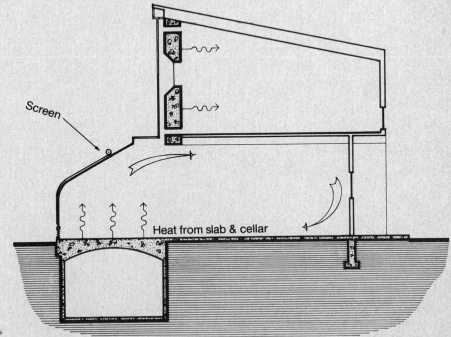

Section B Winter night at greenhouse

125

During the summer months, the house is kept cool by natural air ventilation. Windows on the north side of the house open, letting in cool breezes. The in-coming air creates a suction through the interiors as the hot air rushes out through the vents located beneath the roof eave, at the top of the air space in the Trombe wall.

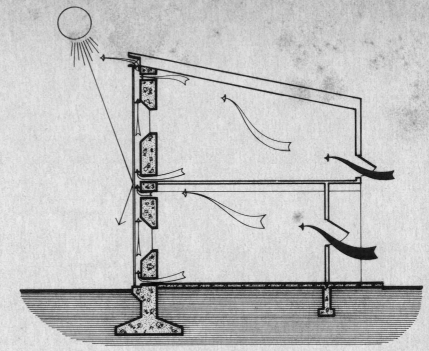

Section A Summer day

A similar pattern is created at the greenhoue side of the house where the top windows of the greenhouse open to aid the outflow of hot air. During the day the screen is kept lowered over the greenhouse walls to avoid an excessive build up of heat inside.

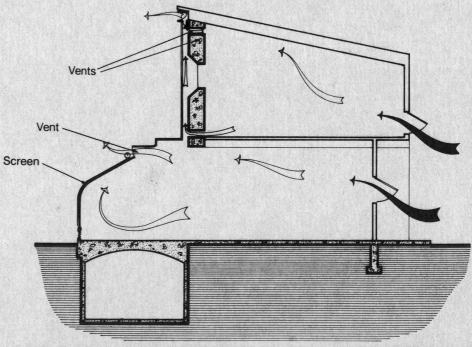

Vents

Vent

Screen

Section B Summer day at greenhouse

From the kitchen, Mrs. Kelbaugh can keep a watchful eye on her son who uses the greenhouse area as an indoor playground.

performed by the entire south-facing, vertical facade of the house, which is double glazed. Behind the glazing is a 6-inch air space. Then comes a 15-inch-thick poured concrete wall that has been treated with a heat-absorbent coating. The concrete Trombe wall extends through every room in the house across the south side, except the bathroom. In each room cool air enters through a vent in the wall at floor level. The air is heated as it rises in the air space between the glazing and the concrete wall. It reenters the room through the vents along the ceiling. Natural convection circulates the air through the room. At night, the massive wall, still warm from the buildup of the day's sun, supplies radiant heat to the rooms.

The greenhouse is also a heat reservoir. It has a thick concrete floor which is warmed by the sun's radiation and then heats both the greenhouse and the cellar below it. The heat is stored in the massive wall as well as the greenhouse floor. About two-thirds of the heating needs of the house come from the sun. This could be increased to 90 percent, Kelbaugh believes, with an insulating shutter to cover the glass wall at night. "We'd make it through the winter with the fireplace only as supplement," he said. But such an insulating shutter would have to be custom-made, and they can't yet invest in one. For the time being, the house relies on backup heat from a gas-fired forced-air furnace, controlled by a thermostat. In a sunnier climate, the solar system could supply 100 percent of the space heating, Kelbaugh believes.

In summer, the Trombe wall helps to keep the house cool by air convection, or the natural law that hot air rises and cool air falls. The cool air enters through vents located on the north side of the house and forces the warm air out through the vents located at the top of the Trombe wall, just beneath the roof eaves on the south side. This powerful air current keeps the masonry wall cool, and it radiates this coolness to the surrounding rooms. The air can also be circulated through the house mechanically with the aid of four small fans located in the attic. To ensure the efficiency of the Trombe-wall system, Kelbaugh was careful to insulate the house well. East, north, and west walls are filled with cellulose fiber injected into the wall cavities under high pressure.

Junius Eddy

"We grow more in awe of the tenuous hold our lives have on this small planet, more convinced that the sun renews us, in an almost religious way."

The wing that Louise and Junius Eddy added on to their house in Little Compton, Rhode Island, is an attempt at total solar heating in a typical New England climate. To brave the rigorous winters and frequent cloudy periods, the Eddys now rely on a Jøtul stove as their only supplementary source of heat.

The 1,500-square-foot addition consists of a living room opening onto a two-story greenhouse, a workshop, a bedroom, and a utility room. On the outside, the southern face of the new wing has an upper story of twenty air-type flat plate solar collectors, rising above the greenhouse walls. Abutting the building are three additional collectors linked to a 65-gallon water tank, which supply 50 percent of their hot water needs.

The concept behind the efficiency of the system is threefold: superior insulation, a combination of solar hardware with nonmechanical use of the structure to trap heat (in this case, via the greenhouse), and a rock storage bin of 1,050 cubic feet capable of holding nine days' worth of heat.

The ambitious project grew out of the Eddys' wish to use their second home on the Rhode Island shoreline year-round. They checked the winter electric rates (the house was then all-electric) and were appalled that they could run bills up to $400 a month. While looking for alternatives, they met Travis Price, who was working on a solar-energy project in New York City (see page 192). Price designed the architectural additions and Everett Barber designed the solar system. They thought about installing an auxiliary electric heat source for the wing, but it would have added an unwarranted amount of money to their budget. Besides, Price hoped to make the structure totally self-suf-

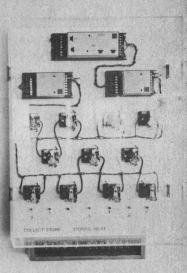

The Eddys' solar collectors rise in a steep slope above a greenhouse, providing a significant addition to an otherwise conventional house overlooking an ocean inlet in Rhode Island. Standing to the right of the house is a separate solar collector which supplies the hot water for the family. The interior of the new greenhouse can be seen above. The panel (right) which controls and monitors the solar heating system is prominently displayed on one of the living room walls. The Eddys' teenaged sons turned the control panel into a graphic art object by painting it in bright colors.

129

ficient through a combination of good insulation, solar hardware, and passive use of the sun's heat via absorbent materials in the house itself. "The greenhouse, which allows direct sunlight to penetrate the house on the south and strike absorptive materials such as the concrete floor and rocks, picks up the missing 20 to 30 percent of heat that a hardware system generally lacks, and eliminates any use of fossil fuels," he explains.

The house is insulated with 3 inches of sprayed polyurethane around the concrete perimeter walls, 3½-inch fiberglass batts, plus 1-inch Styrofoam panels on the outside walls and 6½-inch batts in the roof joists. Tightly sealed double-glazed windows provide additional insulation.

When the local public utility, the Narragansett Electric Company, heard that there would be a solar house in its neighborhood, it offered to meter the house to test "what contribution solar energy could make to a total-electric home in Little Compton, Rhode Island." That was when the Eddys were considering electric baseboard heating as the backup source of heat for their wing. When the utility company heard that a Jøtul stove would be the sole supplementary heat source, its interest evaporated. As Junius Eddy pointed out in a letter to the company, "I found it interesting, and indeed rather ironic, that the promotional tail apparently wags the research dog in a company that already stresses in its advertising how its research activities will lead to savings for customers by using the energy of the sun."

The Eddys started living in the new wing with two of their six children in February 1976, some months before the addition was completely finished. "We didn't realize how drastically it would affect our lives," says Junius Eddy, an educator who serves on the board of trustees of Antioch College and as a consultant to the Rockefeller Foundation. Since the house is on a scenic inlet of the Atlantic shoreline, the Eddys were already attuned to the natural environment, its changing moods and seasonal nuances—they thought.

The Eddys monitored the atmospheric data inside the house daily for a base-year record to refer back to. Their teenage sons, Doug and Jim, built a control panel, which they mounted on the living room wall—"a technological graphic-art object," their father calls it. The panel is brightly colored, and red lights indicate which fan or motorized damper is on, while various thermometers register the temperatures of the indoors, outdoors, the greenhouse, and the rock storage bed.

"We began to notice just how much the outdoor conditions affected our indoor lives—not just how cold or warm we were, but how it influenced our attitude—how we felt," Junius Eddy reported. The family now reacts to every atmospheric change. "We hear a click in the relay on the control switchboard that draws our attention. 'We've stopped collecting,' we say, 'it's clouding up.' Or, 'We're distributing directly, it must be hotter outside than it is in the rock storage pit.' Or, 'The sun's arc is higher in the sky than it was a few months ago, the collection cycle starts earlier each day and turns off in midafternoon.'"

The family's heightened awareness is echoed in the mechanical changes of the house. On the greenhouse windows are skylids—louvers that are from Zomeworks in Albuquerque, which open and close automatically, using no electricity to control the sun's supply of heat inside. They are controlled instead by Freon-filled tubes on the louver edges. As the Freon heats up or cools down, depending upon the strength of the sun's rays, it gasifies, migrates, and opens or closes the louver by gravity. "We look into the greenhouse and watch the skylids closing automatically, one by one and in no particular order," Junius Eddy says, "and we are aware of hot air rising, cold air settling. The switches, relays, and monitoring lights on the control panel remind us that the earth is turning and day is ending."

As so many people who live in solar houses remark, living with the sun registers on the psyche. "It is not just the financial savings. We grow more in awe of the tenuous hold our lives have on this small planet, more convinced that the sun renews us, in an almost religious way," says Junius. "It has made us profoundly grateful that the sun is up there, the center of our universe, warming us up and keeping us alive. That atavistic sense of the elements that early man knew and felt has become a part of our lives."

The old part of the building, with its second-story sun deck can be seen in the photograph above. The Eddys recently added the extension to the right of the original house, which not only gave them additional space, but provided them with a solar heating system. Beside the greenhouse, the new addition holds a living room, workshop, and utility room downstairs, and a bedroom/study upstairs.

Charles and Mary Lou Swift

"A solar clothesline is better than an electric dryer."

Three silos, topped by a 60-foot-long horizontal solar collector, form the unusual design for this New Jersey residence. The circular forms reminded the Swifts of the indigenous architecture of Tanzania, where the couple spent several years. The resemblance was entirely intentional on their part.

When you come back to the United States after eight years in a foreign country, it's hard to find positive forces to identify with," says Mary Lou Swift. One positive force she and her husband, Charles, could identify with in the U.S. was natural energy, and that is how they came to build their unusual silo house in rural New Jersey, near the Delaware River. The Swifts had lived in Tanzania, where Charles was a psychiatric consultant to the Ministry of Health and a professor of psychiatry at the University Medical School in Dar-es-Salaam. "There, the priorities were very different," they say. Here, the concern is increasingly for the environment. "We wanted to be part of the drive, the rhythm, the swell of enthusiasm to use natural energy."

With their designer-builders, Steve Badanes and John Ringel, the Swifts built a house that was inspired by the rural, mud-walled roundhouses they had known in Africa. Theirs, however, is adapted from prefabricated silos, bought from the Unadilla Silo Company of Unadilla, New York. The "house" is three interconnected 20-foot-diameter modules—the one on the west is reserved for sleeping and bathing, the middle one for eating and congregating, and the eastern one for use as a study and shed. Straddling the three roofs is a 60-foot-long, 5-foot-high air-to-rock custom-built solar collector. It's designed to provide about 50 percent of their space heating.

The Swifts, a couple with six grown children, took an active part in the construction of their new home, as did whichever of their children were visiting. The family did most of the interior finishing work. And they dug a 140-foot ditch around the trees in order to bury the unsightly electric and telephone lines. They wouldn't allow a single

Each of the three silos houses a different communal space in the Swifts' household. One (above) is the kitchen and living area, while another (far right) is Mr. Swift's library and studio. The couple stand in front of their house, (center).

tree to be cut; otherwise they could have hired a tractor with a shovel for this herculean task.

The 1,400-square-foot house cost them $56,000 to build. "It was more than we expected to pay," says Charles Swift, "but the total sum included a number of extra expenditures such as the septic field, a gravel roadway, and the landscaping."

It's too early to assess the efficiency of their solar system, which was not in operation as of the time this book went to press. Temporarily, they rely on heat from the wood-burning fireplaces. Only the main bathroom has electric heat.

The designer-builders, Badanes and Ringel, saw their participation in the house as a unique challenge: to incorporate a solar heating system in a strong personal statement. "We all wanted to see how far we could go with solar. And there was a good dialogue between the client and ourselves. It has been an important learning process for us all."

Mary Lou expressed it another way: "In this house we feel close to nature, and being close to the environment is part of the breath of life."

Kent Bloomer

"It's very satisfying to know that the windmill will be working when the power company grid is down. It's self-sufficiency, like having a garden out back."

Kent Bloomer's windmill isn't really operating yet, but it is already a rallying point for the whole community of Leetes Island, a small coastal section of Guilford, Connecticut, which is gaining a reputation as a conservation-minded town. The wind generator stands on top of a 49-foot tower on a clearing near Bloomer's 1840 Federal farmhouse.

Bloomer, a professor of architecture at Yale University, did not erect the windmill to protest against the utility company's rising rates, nor even to save money by generating his own electricity. His home site, which borders an 80-acre clearing of a marine biology preserve, faces into prevailing winds off Long Island Sound. It was ideal for trying out a wind generating system, which he and three Yale students built from scratch out of spare parts, bus alternators, motorcycle chains, pumps, and mill blades.

It took them two and a half weeks to erect the tower and windmill, which was operating for a month or two when a twister came along and demolished it. "The windmill was so badly mangled that it looked like a plane wreck," Bloomer recalls. To his surprise, everyone in town was desolated. "They acted as if someone had died. We couldn't go anywhere without people asking when we would put it up again."

In its short existence, the windmill had won the community's heart as a symbol of self-reliance and the pioneering spirit of rural America. It was up long enough, however, for the Bloomers to realize that a wind system wouldn't make sense economically in their locale, where utility rates were only 5 cents per kilowatt-hour. "But the sentiment of the town was so strong that we decided to rebuild it," Bloomer says. His wife, Nona, also missed the windmill. She used to catch a glimpse of it out the window, and in the afternoon the sun would glance off the blades and send flashes of sunlight that lit up the whole house. Even the locomotives making the run between Boston and New Haven would acknowledge the windmill with a whistle. The Bloomers knew the engineers were signaling it, because when the windmill was

Kent Bloomer and a crew of students from Yale University's School of Architecture are photographed in the process of rebuilding a windmill on his property in Guilford, Connecticut. The first one blew down in a storm. The unusual tower design serves several purposes. The lowest level, rimmed by a bench, is a summertime gazebo (above), while the next higher section contains a sleeping loft for the Bloomer children.

This is the view from the windmill's sleeping loft. From one of the three round windows in the triangular-shaped tower, Mark Bloomer and Alexander Naar gaze across the salt marsh to Long Island Sound.

furled, the trains raced by in silence. "The excitement that the windmill generated was enormous," Kent says.

Bloomer located another windmill, a second-hand Jacobs from the Midwest, through his fellow architect and wind buff, David Sellers. He bought it for $1,500, reconditioning it with new bearings and brushes and a new governor, and got the students to reerect the tower. The students had argued with the professor over the design of the first tower—whether it should be streamlined like the Jacobs itself (a futuristic design from the 1930s) or whether it should look like a Dutch windmill. This time everyone had a say: Nona Bloomer asked for an outdoor deck where the family and friends could enjoy the view of the Sound; the Bloomer children—Mark, twelve, and May, nine—asked for a kind of a treehouse with a sleeping loft; the students designed the wood-slatted bottom section of the tower; and Bloomer insisted on the streamlined steel top section—the "business end," as he puts it. The rebuilt Jacobs presides at the top.

The 32-volt, 1.8-kilowatt wind generator is designed to supply the Bloomers' hot water needs. Locating spare parts for the old machine is always a problem. Although the Jacobs units are incredibly reliable, one of their weak points is wear along the teeth of the governor, which causes the tail to wobble. In short order the machine went through two governors. By an amazing fluke, Sellers came across a brand-new Jacobs governor in a hardware store in Nebraska, under an inch of cobwebs, where it had sat on the shelf for three decades. It still had the protective coating on the teeth; he bought it and resold it to Bloomer.

Using a wind generator to supply hot water is a simple process: the current from the generator goes directly to a heating element in the water tank. Bloomer estimates that his hot water heater consumes about 40 percent of his entire electrical load. Bloomer estimates that he will be able to generate 140 kilowatt-hours per month at the very minimum, or 10 percent of what the machine is capable of delivering. Running at 100 percent capacity in a constant 25-mile-an-hour wind (highly unlikely), the machine would generate 1,400 kilowatt-hours per month. The Jacobs will not produce electricity in winds with velocities less than 9 miles per hour.

The system isn't operating yet because Bloomer is in the process of accumulating more funds. What started out as an investment of $300 has mushroomed into nearly $3,000 thus far. He spent $1,500 for the Jacobs, $350 for the steel in the tower (some of the I-beams were recycled from a razed telephone company building in New Haven), and $750 for the lumber in the tower. "It will take me eighty years to pay back my initial investment," Bloomer says. A comparable system brand-new would cost about $8,000. "If you compare this to a hobby or an art form, then it doesn't sound so expensive," he reasons. "Look at how much people spend on hi-fi equipment or sailboats."

"I think what really won hearts up here aesthetically," says Bloomer, "is the windmill's wood bottom that looks like a corncrib and the Buck Rogers top. It's futuristic and nostalgic in one throw." Apparently, the town senses it. "This part of Connecticut is gaining a reputation for conservation, just as New Canaan, Connecticut, had a reputation in the 1950s for houses by the best-known modern architects," Bloomer says. The windmill symbolizes a growing movement in the area. "And it is a beautiful thing to see a windmill facing into a stiff wind, its tail poised like an arrow," he adds. "Way down deep it's very satisfying to know that the windmill will be working when the power company grid is down. It's self-sufficiency, like having a garden out back."

William W. Smith III

Bill Smith is seen against the backdrop of the wind generator that he built to power his small homestead in Jamestown, Rhode Island (right). Smith's wind system took a year or two of trial and error but finally functions satisfactorily.

"Rather than write about energy conservation, I'd better do it."

William W. Smith III, a twenty-eight-year-old ex-Peace Corps member with a Harvard degree in literature, is waging his battle for energy conservation on two fronts—on the socio-political front as a citizens' activist for a safe environment, and on the personal one in his own backyard. He works with dozens of conservation groups such as the Rhode Island Committee on Energy, the Environmental Coalition on Nuclear Power, and the American Littoral Society. He is also busy constructing a 60-foot tower of galvanized steel for his reclaimed Jacobs wind generator. It is temporarily mounted atop a pole made out of beach driftwood, scrap-yard wires, and government-surplus cables. A homemade solar collector supplies his hot water.

"I was writing booklets and pamphlets for energy conservation groups, and I thought, Rather than write about it, I'd better do it," he says. So in 1972 he moved from his hometown of Philadelphia to his father's summer home, a 1917 cottage in Jamestown, Rhode Island. "The state has an excellent wind climate," he explains, "and it's really a nice place to live."

Bill began by building his own wind generator from scratch, but the wobbly two-bladed machine did not work. His second attempt fared only slightly better after a year of tinkering with it. Then he learned about the Jacobs machines that supplied midwestern farmers with reliable power through the 1930s and 1940s. "I didn't realize that I was trying to reinvent what had been in production over thirty years ago," he explained.

Bill took a ten-day trip to the Midwest and, by word of mouth, located a thirty-year-old Jacobs wind generator in Minnesota. Produced up until the 1950s, the machine is now in great demand and highly prized because of its reliability. Jacobs machines have been known to run for thirty years on their original brushes and, in Smith's opinion, will run for another thirty with new brushes and revarnishing. "When you find one that's still on its tower, it's almost sure to work," he says. Unfortunately, the machines were favorite shotgun targets of the local boys and many have been

damaged beyond repair. Smith paid $650 for his machine, then trucked it back to Jamestown, where he made a new set of 13-foot blades for it and fitted it with a new hub and "feathering" mechanism, a safety feature that turns the blades into the wind during storms. He currently has $1,500 invested in his system.

The wind generator currently produces 300 to 400 kilowatt hours per month, or just about what he needs to run his house. "Before the machine was operating, my electricity bills were running about $25 to $30 per month," Bill says. Now the Jacobs produces all his power. A series of batteries from a forklift truck stores the electricity for four days' use. In case of windless days, rare in this part of Rhode Island where the winds are among the strongest on the East Coast, Smith has a standby gasoline generator.

Most wind-generated electricity produces DC current that must be converted to AC for standard home use. Bill has figured out ways to use DC current directly wherever he can—for instance, bypassing the transformer on his radio and replacing the motors on his band saw, drill press, and power lathe for those using DC current. For the refrigerator and freezer, Bill uses a rotary inverter although he finds that it requires an amount of power disproportionate to what it actually produces.

Smith's goal is to build an electronic solid-state inverter that will enable him to sell his wind-produced electricity surplus back to the public power company. In high winds, the inverter would pump the excess electricity into the power company grid and would operate like a temporary "bank loan" for electric power. Smith would draw the utility's power "on credit" when he runs short, returning it to the power company when his wind machine generates the excess. The local utility, Newport Electric, agreed to consider the arrangement, but only when convinced of the safety and reliability of the procedure.

Such inverters are relatively new on the market but, so far, are expensive. One complete system including the inverter tower and windmill cost its

owner $8,000. It does eliminate the need for storage battery systems, required by most home generators, and would make wind-generated electricity infinitely more attractive and practical for the individual home owner.

Bill's ardent support of alternate energy is a full-time commitment. A stream of letters flows out of the tiny office that adjoins his workshop, to senators, legislators, and government officials. As secretary of the Rhode Island Committee on Energy, he was in charge of the mailing campaign during its court challenge of a proposed plan to build a nuclear power plant in nearby Charlestown. Just as avidly, he supports the Offshore Wind Power System (OWPS) proposed by Professor William Heronemus of the University of Massachusetts. It would be a cluster of floating 340-foot-tall wind towers (each carrying three 100-foot blades) strung across Nantucket Shoals, which would supply all of the electricity for New England. The system would supply power for the cities, where individual windmill systems like Smith's would be impractical.

"Three centuries ago, New Englanders on Cape Cod, Long Island Sound, and Narragansett Bay harnessed the wind to drive gristmills and to pump water," Smith said. But now, he feels, no one in government or the power industry is seriously considering wind power for New England. The government and corporations have a stated bias toward nuclear power. "Perhaps it's up to the common people of New England to pester their elected representatives until some action is initiated," he said. That's where most of his own energy is directed.

Neil Welliver

"You feel like a kid with a giant pinwheel."

It is coincidental that two early advocates of wind power, Henry Clews and Neil Welliver, live near the gusty coast of northeastern Maine, within 40 miles of each other. Even more coincidental, they first heard of one another by way of southeastern Australia.

In 1972, both had been in touch with the Quirks Victory Light Company in Sydney, New South Wales, to purchase wind generating equipment. Welliver had seen the firm's advertisement in the *Whole Earth Catalog*. When he made a hasty telephone call to Quirks in Australia to order a 110-volt Dunlite generator and a 50-foot tower on which to mount it, he was told that neighbor Henry Clews had also just placed an order for wind equipment. The two purchases were scheduled to arrive in Boston on the same ship, so Welliver loaned Clews his truck to pick up the equipment for both of them.

Neil Welliver, a well-known artist, had dreamed of building a self-sufficient house for years. When he bought an old farm in Lincolnville, Maine, near the rural landscapes that are frequently the subject of his paintings, he began exploring the various possibilities of natural energy. Inadvertently, the Central Maine Power Company convinced him he had no alternative. The house had no electricity. When Welliver asked the utility

Neil and Polly Welliver have two working wind generators on their farm in northeastern Maine. Neil, an artist, even has enough electricity to power the 600-watt floodlights in his large painting studio (below).

A bank of Century batteries stores the Wellivers' wind-generated electricity. The family also has a Clivus Multrum organic toilet and a gray water filter. The large drum of the filter is located in the control room at the right.

company how much it would cost to run a line 1½ miles from the main road to the house, he was quoted $10,000—more than what he paid for both the house and the land.

Neil tried alternate solutions for power: propane gas for lighting and a propane generator to supply electricity, but the latter required too much maintenance to be practical. Furthermore, the quality of light was inadequate for Welliver's studio. Then he decided that a wind generator would be the answer to both his feud with the power company and his need for electricity. After telephoning to Australia, however, he realized that he hadn't checked whether there was enough wind crossing his land to run it. He was relieved when the local weather bureau reported that his location received an average wind of 12 miles per hour, enough to run the generator.

Welliver and an electrician friend set up the Dunlite wind generating system in ten days, and after a trial run, it was supplying 200 kilowatt-hours of electricity per month. However, the generator could not power the 600-watt floodlights Neil needed for his studio.

Welliver realized he needed a second wind plant, which he bought from Henry Clews. It was a Swiss-made, 6-kilowatt Electro. To beef up his storage capacity, he added fifty-five Century batteries. Combined, the two wind generators now supply 600 to 650 kilowatt-hours of electricity per month to the Welliver household and studio, enough to maintain such appliances as a vacuum cleaner, television, power tools, and refrigerator.

Soon after the wind generating system was operating smoothly, a fire destroyed the farmhouse and also scorched the Dunlite wind generator and weakened the tower so that it had to be replaced. The Wellivers were undaunted by this setback—they decided to rebuild everything. To duplicate their early nineteenth-century farm-

house complex, they located a group of similar buildings that were being dismantled: a house, a barn, and connecting buildings. They were bought for under $1,000 and were then dismantled, moved, and put back together on Welliver's site. The new house was insulated with a relatively new process, using urea formaldehyde, an organic compound, which is foam applied with a hose; having the consistency of shaving cream when applied, it is capable of filling all the crevices. A depth of 4 inches of the material is held to be the equivalent of 7 to 8 inches of fiberglass insulation. The roof was insulated with Styrofoam panels.

Additional energy-saving features Welliver incorporated into the house include a Clivus Multrum organic toilet and a gray-water filter located in the battery storage room. The filter is a 4-foot-diameter cone of fiberglass, filled with crushed stone: it filters the waste water from sinks and showers and recycles the water for use in the garden, which grows most of the family's vegetables. The Wellivers also have a root cellar, which keeps their produce fresh through the winter and spring.

Replacing their damaged Dunlite wind generator is a rebuilt Jacobs wind generator. Somehow, the Swiss Electro was unharmed by the blaze and continues to function. However, Welliver warns, it does not work well on low wind speeds and is structurally inadequate to tolerate gusty high winds. On the other hand, the American-made Jacobs wind generator, he finds, is very reliable.

Welliver's system produces an AC current that is transformed into DC by diodes inside the generator, which is then carried by wires from the tower to a control panel in the basement of the house. From there it can be channeled either directly into an appliance that is switched on at the time or to the storage batteries for future use. When the batteries are fully charged and when no power is being drawn, a voltage regulator reduces the output of the generator to safeguard the batteries from damage by overcharging. The bank of storage batteries also helps to stabilize the fluctuations in the current caused by wind variations.

The entire Welliver family—Neil, his wife, Polly, and their four children—are aware that their energy supply is tuned to the weather conditions. "Even the kids remember to turn out the lights behind them," Neil notes. The steady whirring of the generator blades and the shadows they project onto the house are a source of satisfaction. "The wind plant is 25 percent energy-producing and 75 percent pleasure," he says. "You feel like a kid with a giant pinwheel."

Welliver admits to a rebellious streak, typical of the American pioneer. He is a member of the advisory board of Safe Power for Maine, an anti-nuclear group organized to halt plans for a nuclear power plant at Sears Island, Maine. He even placed an advertisement in eight Maine newspapers, paid for by himself, protesting the invasion of "our every right by big government and big corporations." Economics are not at the heart of his determination to be independent of the utility company. Polly Welliver sums it all up when she says, "It was not really the money that caused us to put up the wind generator. We are really doing all of this out of perversity."

Michael Reynolds

"I try everything out on my buildings. My designs are a conglomeration of many ideas about recycling materials and saving energy."

The owner of this unique house, an architect-builder, experimented with construction materials and techniques. The addition at the left of the photograph, for instance, was built largely out of recycled water-filled beer cans.

In 1971, Michael Reynolds, an architect-builder in Taos, New Mexico, watched Walter Cronkite on a television program deplore the way Americans litter the highways with beer cans. Suddenly an idea took hold of him: Why not recycle the cans and use them as a building material? He figured there were about three million homes built every year, and he calculated that one-fifth of them could be built out of the eighteen billion beer cans that are produced annually.

Recycling materials was still very much in the air then. Reynolds recruited the local Boy Scouts to round up used cans and asked bartenders to save cans for him to pick up each morning. Reynolds (who is no relation to anyone at Reynolds Aluminum Corporation) experimented with dozens of ways to use the cans as building materials: making walls out of them by stacking them vertically and horizontally; filling them with mortar; making six-pack building blocks by baling them together with wire. Almost by accident Reynolds discovered that the air space in the cans makes them a good insulator.

As time wore on, Reynolds became intrigued with the idea of using beer cans as solar heat sinks. Because they are considerably smaller than the 55-gallon oil drums usually employed as solar water tanks, it takes much less time for the water-filled cans to heat up when exposed to the sun's rays. Although he had been using steel beer cans for their strength, the relatively newer aluminum cans turned out to be superior heat conductors when filled with water. Reynolds then commissioned a Denver brewer to fill unused aluminum cans with carbonated water, leaving a small air-space to allow for expansion. Not only were cans cheaper than rocks for solar heat storage, he

decided, but they were also more efficient: According to Reynolds, they require only one-fourth the total square-foot area needed by rocks to maintain the same amount of solar heat. To prove his theory, Reynolds decided to add on to his house a solar-collector greenhouse as an auxiliary heat source. It took more than a thousand 16-ounce cans to complete it. The greenhouse has a floor of upright cans set in mortar. Electric cables are laced under the upright cans in the greenhouse floor to supplement the solar heat. With the addition of the solar greenhouse, the Reynoldses claim that they only have to use their conventional electric baseboard heaters on the coldest of nights. Taos, a 7,000-foot-altitude town, has rigorous winters and cool summer nights. Susan Reynolds figures that they save 50 percent of their heating costs, or between $40 and $50 a month, during the winter with the beer can greenhouse. They also grow vegetables year-round, and their young son uses the greenhouse as a playroom.

Susan and Jack Crowl

"We had to convince the banks to finance the first house made out of beer cans...now they treat them like any other house out here."

ichael Reynolds went on to design and build other houses out of beer cans, and today there are eight in all. He refined the technique considerably in the design of the small, 625-square-foot house for Susan and Jack Crowl in Des Montes, New Mexico. The structure is basically one large room with a greenhouse attached on the south facade. Inside, there are two small interior divisions, an alcove on the northwest corner for sleeping and another alcove on the northeast corner to hold a kitchenette. Architect Reynolds made provision for future expansion by extending the roof and the north wall to form a carport that the Crowls can eventually close off to make into an additional room.

In a design feature similar to the one on Reynolds's own house, the greenhouse on the Crowl house acts as the solar collector, trapping the sunlight and raising the air temperature inside the enclosure. When the window between the greenhouse and the living room is opened, the heated

Stacked beer cans form both the interior and exterior walls of this house in New Mexico, seen from the outside (left) and inside (above). The living area opens onto a greenhouse angled toward the sun's rays which also helps to heat the interiors of the house.

air flows into the house to warm the interiors. The sunlight hitting the back wall of the greenhouse warms up that surface, which retains the heat until evening, when it is radiated back into the house. In addition, the greenhouse creates an insulated buffer between the indoors and the outdoors.

All four walls of the building are constructed with two layers of stacked beer cans, laid on their sides, with sheets of Styrofoam insulation panel sandwiched in between. The walls are about 1 foot thick, creating a thick thermal mass. The stacked cans facing the interior of the house are filled with water three-quarters of the way; the cans facing the exterior are empty. "The principle is that of a heat sink," says Reynolds. "On a clear day the water in the cans may reach 115 degrees with the sun beating down on them and then stay warm for hours to heat the interior spaces at night." As an auxiliary source of heat, electric cables are threaded beneath additional beer cans, which are embedded in the concrete floor of the house. This backup heat source is used only three

or four days all winter long, the architect claims.

The rest of the house is exceptionally well insulated, too. The ceiling has 9 inches of fiberglass insulation, and the north wall is banked by a high mound of earth. In addition, a small vestibule provides an air cushion between the outside and the back entry door. To keep the interiors cool in summer, Reynolds designed a roof overhang on the south side of the building which shades the house during the day.

Reynolds reports that the house costs only a little more than one built of conventional wood framing but that it has several advantages over the latter for reducing heating bills. The extra expenses went primarily for the extra insulation and for the water-filled beer cans, which had to be custom-made at a nearby brewery. However, the Crowls had no trouble getting conventional financing from the First Northern Savings and Loan Association. "We had to convince the banks to finance the first house made out of beer cans," Reynolds says, "but now they treat them like any other house out here."

The Crowls built their house on a very modest budget. Despite its unconventional appearance, the water-filled beer cans give the house superior insulating qualities, affording them considerable savings in fuel.

John Gale

"It's the happiest house we've ever lived in."

John Gale was impressed by Michael Reynolds's use of beer can construction and decided to build his own aluminum beer can house in Taos, New Mexico. Gale knew about the heating and cooling benefits of solar house design, because he had lived in traditional adobe houses where the only supplementary heat source, a fireplace built into the corner of the living room, was usually adequate to heat the whole house. He had also built an A-frame house with a glass front facing south. He knew from that experience that the morning sunlight entering the windows was enough to heat the interiors and trigger the thermostat to shut down the furnace by eleven o'clock in the morning, even in the dead of winter.

John and his wife, Georgia, built their house with their own hands, using an estimated thirty thousand beer cans in the process. Following the example of their mentor, Reynolds, the Gales hired the children in the area to collect empty cans, and they purchased empties from local taverns for 12 to 16 cents a pound.

The Gales incorporated the beer cans into the construction of the house in a somewhat different fashion from Reynolds's method. They used them to create thick, insulating walls—in effect, a thermal shell not unlike adobe. The frame of the building is conventional post-and-beam construction, used in nearly all residential building design. The beer cans were then used to fill the spaces between the studs. Two layers of cans are separated by 2 inches of rigid polyurethane foam insulation. The cans are stacked in rows and banded together with concrete mortar. The windows are all double thickness, insulating glass.

John Gale's house (left) incorporates the beer can construction technique in a conventional frame building. He estimates that he used 30,000 beer cans for this 1,500 square-foot house.

The interiors of the Gale house are bright and airy. The ends of the cans, embedded in the walls, make a distinctive pattern over the interior wall surfaces. Wood roof beams and structural posts were left exposed and these, too, lend warmth to the rooms. The master bedroom, like the living room below it, has a magnificent view of the Sangre de Cristo mountains .

The beer can walls proved to be superior for heat retention. The Gales' electric bills, even in the dead of winter when temperatures drop to 10 degrees, average under $25 per month. (It costs about $150 per month to heat a conventional house in their immediate area.) For occasional supplementary heat, the concrete floors of the house are inlaid with electric cables, turning the slab into a source of radiant heat.

The Gales are pleased with both the house and its operation. Maintenance, they say, is negligible. "It's the happiest house we have ever lived in," John says, "with the sun streaming through the living room window all winter long and our fabulous view of the Sangre de Cristo Mountains in the distance." The Gales estimate that their 1,530-square-foot house cost them about $38,000, excluding the cost of the land, the well, and the septic tank, and the money saved through the couple's own labor. "It is an ecological house," John adds, "built by cleaning up the environment, and yet it is acceptable to people who are accustomed to conventional standards of living."

Douglas Boleyn

"If we exploited our solar resources, we could cut down dramatically on nuclear expansion."

Aside from the solar collectors on the roof, the Douglas Boleyns' house in Gladstone, Oregon, looks like a conventional, medium-priced, cedar-shingled residence in a typical suburban setting. Douglas Boleyn, an electrical engineer, wanted to include as many energy-conserving features as he could in the envelope of his three-bedroom, two-story house. It was designed for maximum insulation. The glass windows are all double glazed, and the north side of the house is almost free of fenestration. Midway through the design of the house, Boleyn was given a grant to go solar. "We asked the architects to set the roof angle at 60 degrees to accommodate equipment for collectors. Since the basement was large enough to hold the water storage tanks, there wasn't much else to change."

The cost of additional insulation added less than $1,500 to the overall initial cost of the house, about $35,500 not including the land. What was expensive was the solar equipment. While everything about the house looks conventional, it isn't. As Boleyn explained, it evolved into an experimental and demonstration research project, undertaken by the Portland General Electric Company, for whom Boleyn is the energy management consul-

The top-of-the-hill array of solar collectors mounted on Douglas Boleyn's roof is the only visible difference from that of his neighboring houses in this typical suburban Oregon setting (below). Up close (left), the three-bedroom house is a handsome addition to the community.

tant. The $30,000 solar system, financed by PGE, included the cost of the collectors and storage tanks, installation, engineering, consultation, and the extra hours incurred by union laborers unfamiliar with solar heating hardware. PGE also supplied all of the instrumentation and made computer readouts for data analysis to check performance.

PGE is a private utility supplying about 40 percent of the electricity to the state of Oregon. It already has one nuclear plant in operation but is

sensitive to growing public apprehension about this method of energy production. "If we exploited our full solar resources," says Boleyn, "we could cut down dramatically on nuclear expansion."

So, with an appropriation earmarked for solar exploration, Portland General Electric is making use of the Boleyn house in their public information and educational programs. While demonstrating different modes of solar heating suitable for the Pacific Northwest, PGE is also showing

The interiors (left) are soothingly decorated with modern furniture. A free-standing fireplace separates the living room from the dining area. The local utility company Portland General Electric, supplied the monitoring equipment (below) that analyzes the performance of the solar system. Sharing space in the same room is the heavily insulated water tank.

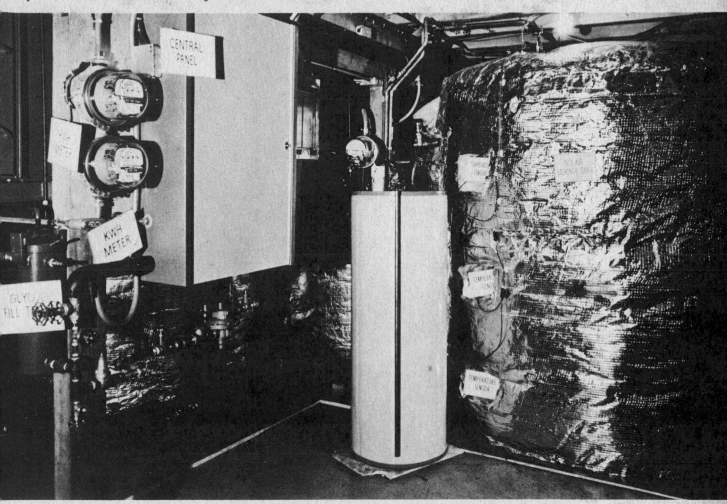

how solar heat can be utilized compatibly alongside an electric utility. They foresee solar systems as a way to supplement electrical energy during peak periods, and they reason that off-peak electrical energy can supplement the solar contribution.

Born and raised in the Portland area, Boleyn has long been aware of the realities of the Oregon climate and weather, and the difficulties of using solar energy there. He has also been concerned about the environment and classifies himself as a progressive who sees the need for continuing public education in this important field. The state of Oregon, too, is relatively enlightened on the subject and has granted a property-tax break for the value added to a building by a solar heating system.

Boleyn's solar system provides about one-third of the space heating in midwinter; by early spring it produces half of the house's heat. In such a climate, where winters are long and cloudy, even this supplementary source is significant.

163

Toby Richards

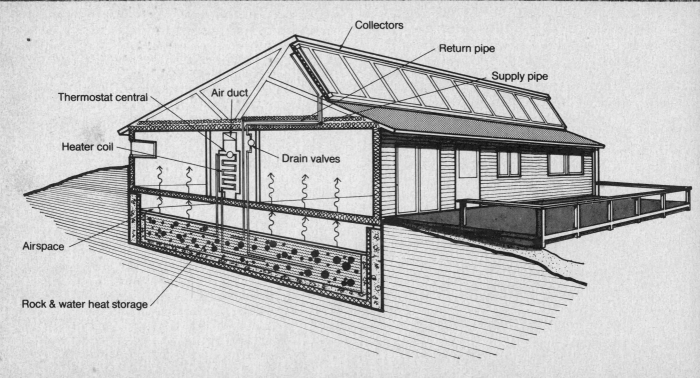

Collectors

Return pipe

Supply pipe

Thermostat central

Air duct

Heater coil

Drain valves

Airspace

Rock & water heat storage

"We keep the temperature at 72 degrees all winter—and who else can afford to do that nowadays?"

Carol and Toby Richards are in the front rank of what could become thousands of Americans to live in solar-heated development houses. Their "solar ranch," which they bought for $35,000, is a demonstration model for Solar Homes, Inc., a Jamestown, Rhode Island, developer. It is a typical one-level ranch house, in the developer's vernacular (there are plans for a solar Cape Cod and a solar mansard as well), except that it adheres to fuel-saving principles. Most of the windows face south, there is only one small window on the north, and the building has superior insulation.

The Richardses, both of whom teach at Notre Dame High School in Central Falls, Rhode Island, saw the developer's "Open House" sign while out on a drive. "Being science teachers, we were aware of solar energy and believed in energy conservation," says Toby Richards. "Whether the fuel crisis was a put-up job or not, it was a warning of things to come." They looked at the house, liked it, and bought it. The first house they ever owned, it has 960 square feet of living space that includes two bedrooms and an attached two-car garage.

Solar Homes, Inc., tried out various natural-energy heating systems before settling on this one. The company has a binful of discarded valves, gauges, pumps, and spare parts to attest to their lengthy trial-and-error period. "We wanted a system that we could sell to the average consumer and feel confident that it was reliable enough not to bring complaints," says Spencer Dickinson, one of the company's co-owners and a representative to the Rhode Island Legislature.

The water-type solar collectors the company ended up using are individual prefabricated panels of copper, with copper tubing bonded to them, that can be fastened directly to the plywood sheathing on the roof, which is angled at 57 degrees. The collectors are covered with Kalwall fiberglass sheeting. The collectors drain automatically under freezing conditions. Water is both the heating vehicle and the storage medium, flowing down from the collectors to a 10,000-gallon storage tank beneath the house. Solar Homes, Inc., preferred this water system with automatic drainage to a closed-loop, permanently filled antifreeze system because they found it more efficient.

The water storage tank is calculated to be large enough to carry the house through the longest period of cloudy New England weather, and the company claims it has a thirty-day storage capacity. "We needed a device for extracting heat out of storage at a controlled rate," says Dickinson, "and that device is a water-to-air heat pump." When used with a large water storage tank, the pump draws heat from storage electrically to provide space heating and hot water by moving heat via compressors from the storage tank into a hot water heater. The advantage of the heat pump is that it is reversible and that it can provide air conditioning in the warm months. Because it runs on electricity, the cost of operating the system is reflected in the utility bills. Solar Homes, Inc., estimated that the average heating bill is only 6 cents a day most of the year. However, it jumps to 75 cents a day during the coldest days of January, when the backup electric heat source is operating full-time.

The Richardses claim that they are never short of heat, even during a recent particularly severe winter for the Eastern Seaboard. "People are surprised at how warm the house is," Toby says. "We keep the temperature at 72 degrees all winter—and who else can afford to do that nowadays?" Because theirs is a custom-made prototype, the Richardses were able to purchase it at a special price by agreeing to let the developer use it as a model home. The solar hardware on the Richardses' house cost the developer about $8,000. Solar Homes, Inc., is now accepting orders for similar house models that sell for about $65,000.

Looking quite conventional from the outside, this ranch-style developer's house hides a functioning solar heating plant. Beneath the house is a tank filled with water and rocks. It is the main heat storage facility for the sun-heated water from the solar collectors mounted on the roof. Heat from the rock-water bin radiates up through an airspace and then through the floor, turning it into a radiant slab. In addition, heated air is carried through ducts to warm the rooms. During a cloudy spell, a heat pump is activated to supply stored hot air to the house interiors.

Mobile Solar Home

"It's the first solar-heated mobile home in the country."

Los Alamos, the site of the development of the first atom bomb in the 1940s, is now the site of the country's first solar-heated mobile home. The prototype, financed by the federal Energy Research and Development Administration (ERDA), is now being tested before going into production. With an estimated 18 percent of the single-family-home market in this country made up of mobile homes, a solar-heated model could have a considerable impact on energy conservation. The unit, a modular version of the typical mobile home, was designed and built by architects Burns and Peters, engineers from ISE, Inc., and contractors from A.W.I. Builders, Inc., all of Albuquerque, New Mexico, under the direction of Los Alamos Scientific Laboratories' Dr. J. Douglas Balcomb. The prototype cost $40,000 to build, Dr. Balcomb reports, but he predicts that mass production will reduce the figure to the $25,000 range.

The revolutionary mobile home consists of two modular units, each measuring 12 feet wide by 44 feet long (or double the size of the average mobile home). It has conventional wood-frame construction and is insulated with 3⅝ inches of fiberglass insulation and 1-inch-thick Styrofoam board. The front face of the unit carries an array of 340

The prototype for a solar-heated mobile home is straightforward in design. Solar collectors form the entire south-facing side. The heat storage unit is a series of pint glass jars, filled with water, and stacked in the utility room.

The floor plan of the mobile unit is quite like that of a modest home. The house is more accurately a "modular" home because it consists of two units that join in the center.

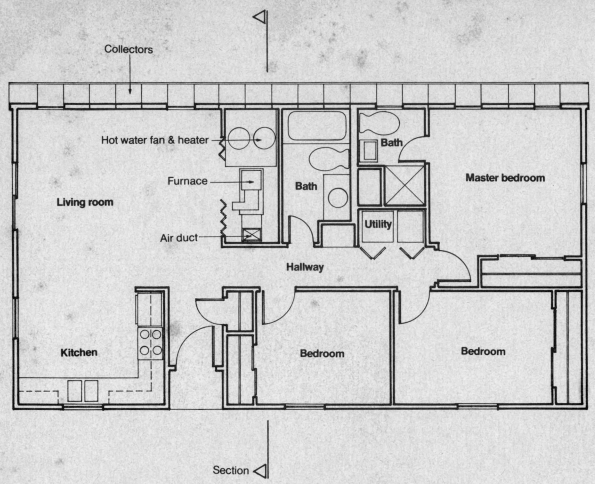

Collectors

Hot water fan & heater

Furnace

Living room

Air duct

Bath

Bath

Utility

Master bedroom

Kitchen

Hallway

Bedroom

Bedroom

Section

square feet of solar collectors, angled at 60 degrees. Perhaps the most unusual feature of the mobile home is its method of heat storage—a 10-by-6-foot wall area in the living room filled with 1,536 pint-glass jars. Each jar is filled three-quarters of the way with water to allow a gap for expansion in freezing climes. The ERDA fact sheet, which describes the storage system as a "water bundle," says that it holds approximately 190 gallons of water. "The system is quite simple," explains Stanley Moore, the project engineer. "The sun heats the air in the collector. The air flows through the stacked bottles and warms them up to anywhere between 100 and 150 degrees. When the sun goes down, the process reverses

itself. A small blower conducts the cooling air inside the trailer through the warmed jars. The air picks up heat from them, and is then distributed through ducts around the trailer."

According to Moore, the solar heat system supplies 75 percent of the space-heating load and 85 percent of the hot water supply. The trailer is equipped with an electric furnace as an auxiliary heating system, but Moore has no estimates yet for how much electricity will be needed to run the furnace. (The electric blower, he contends, will cost only a few dollars per month to run.) The mobile home must be tested first in other climates before regular production of the unit can be scheduled.

Because of the need for a highly reliable, mass-produced house, the solar heat system is more complicated than many other designs. There are electrically operated boosters to help out in cloudy periods, such as the auxiliary heating element for the house's hot water supply and a standby electric hot air-furnace.

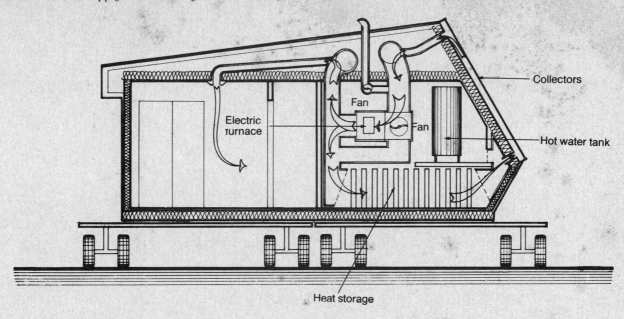

Under sunny conditions, air flows from the collectors and charges the heat storage unit. To heat the rooms, air can be directed into them directly from the heat storage. Fans and dampers control the direction of the air flow. When the collectors are not operating, the house can draw heat directly from the storage bin. Blowers pull the air past the hot water jars to the electric hot-air furnace where it is boosted to the right temperature, if needed, and directed into the rooms.

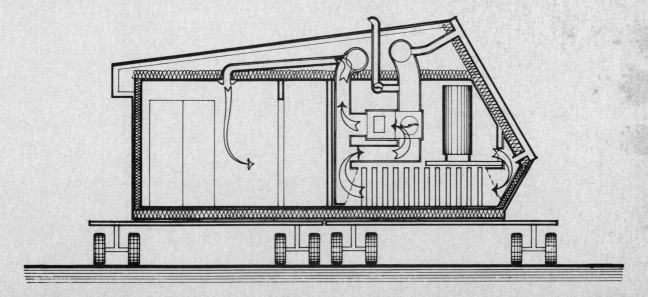

Jonathan Hammond

"I took a look around and realized that very little was being done to change the outdated and wasteful building methods."

Davis, California, a town of thirty thousand people 40 miles east of San Francisco, is the first city in the United States to pass a building code for community energy conservation. The code is due largely to the efforts of an environmentalist team coordinated by landscape architect Jonathan Hammond, meteorologist Marshall Hunt, architect Richard Cramer, and engineer L. W. Neubauer. They spent two years of intensive research, of educating the public and getting the community involved, and in 1975 the City Council passed Ordinance No. 784, which governs such things in new house construction as the amount of window area permitted, the roof color, and quality of insulation.

Jonathan Hammond has been an advocate of energy conservation since his college days. "There were a lot of people studying ecosystems then," he recalls, "but I was more interested in human ecology." He lives with his wife, Lorie, and their two children in a sixty-year-old house in Winters, California. In 1972 he converted it for solar heat. The house now has a south-facing wall of thirty stacked oil drums, filled with 15,000 pounds of water, and its solar system is based on the same principle that heats the Steve Baer house in Corrales, New Mexico (page 44). Attached to the house is a separate 50-square-foot collector that heats the 80-gallon water tank for the family's hot water supply.

Hammond recalls, "I took a look around and realized that very little was being done to change the outdated and wasteful building methods." It was then that he organized the team of his friends and colleagues and studied current building methods, siting, fenestration, building materials, and analyzed how they contributed to energy use. They formulated the provisions for the building code, and persuaded a local builder and friend,

Jon Hammond's 60-year-old house in Davis, California, is a good example of one family's attempt at self-sufficient living. The Hammonds make maximum use of their small backyard by maintaining a vegetable garden off their patio. A freestanding solar collector to the left of the house supplies the family with its hot water.

Hammond also remodeled the house for solar heating. He used water-filled oil barrels (below) as heat sinks. These are stacked in rows in front of the new south-facing windows. The new skylights (below, right), were added to the house to bring additional light into the interiors. The Franklin stove is the house's sole source of supplementary winter heat.

Mike Corbett, to try them out on a house to show other builders and architects that their suggested performance requirements were practical and would not add appreciably to building costs.

The code's most important provision is "southernization," or orienting the house toward the south and using a roof overhang to keep out the high summer sun but let in the low winter sun. The code also upgrades insulation requirements, limits window areas to 12½ percent of the floor area (except on the south side or where double-insulating glass is used), restricts unshaded glass, and regulates roof color so that no colors darker than four on the Munsell color scale (a standard color code chart) may be used. Now the city of Davis has started work on a neighborhood-planning ordinance to encourage subdivisions with better pedestrian and bicycle access, narrower streets, more usable land, and landscaping designed to improve the climate.

Other California communities are watching with interest the results of the Davis building code. Hammond's group, incorporated as Living Systems, now specializes in the contracting of other energy conservation projects. Sacramento County and the city of Indio have already retained their services. "If other communities in the state adopted a similar energy conservation code," says Jon Hammond, "there would be a savings of at least 5 percent in California's present energy consumption."

Not everyone agrees with Hammond's assessment. One architect pointed out that such a literal law might merely be replacing one set of restrictions with another. He suggests that criteria for new buildings based on performance might make a more creative ordinance. For instance, rather than stipulating how much and where windows should be placed or how large they should be, the overall energy consumption of a building should be regulated. The method and design features used to meet those requirements would be left to the ingenuity of the architect, builder, or engineer and would leave room for innovation and technological refinements not yet developed or considered.

On a personal level, Jon Hammond's own energy consumption has been drastically reduced since installing his home solar heating system. The weather in Davis ranges in temperature from a high of 100 degrees to a low of 53 degrees in summer and averages 45 degrees in winter. The first winter their system was used, the Hammonds burned one-third of a cord of wood in their wood stove, the only backup heat source, and the following winter, "even less than that."

Ecotope

"And they see that a great many things are possible under the sun."

Ecotope is a focus of environmental action in the Pacific Northwest. It is a community of like-minded people, a research group, a nonprofit educational facility, and a consortium of concerned individuals from many walks of life. Its concern, said Howdy Reichmuth, a former nuclear submarine physicist who now prefers to build solar greenhouses with the group, is with the "whole question": how to live responsibly. "It's a getting together, an alignment of beautiful·possibilities—gardening, sewage management, water and wind use, natural heat and energy." The Ecotope group, codirected by Ken Smith and Evan Brown, has a base in a lovely Victorian mansion in Seattle, called PRAG (Public Research Assistance Group) and also an organic farm, called Pragtree, in the country some 40 miles away, which is run by Woody and Becky Deryckx and Davis Straub. Both the house and the farm, in Arlington, Washington, are part of a nonprofit land trust.

The group is also associated with other projects, including the magazine *Rain*, published by Lee Johnson in Portland, Oregon. "We work with anyone who wants a lifestyle in harmony with nature, a decentralized, low-impact, nonexploitative society," says Ken Smith. That consciousness is well received in the Northwest—in the food co-ops, among small-business people, union members, old socialists, and even by public utilities, Ecotope's members have found. "Since the 1960s, a vision of energy conservation has grown," Smith continues. "The vast resources wasted in the Vietnam War while millions starved explicated the problem. Now we have moved from antiwar to environmental activism."

The group is both active and visible. At Pragtree, Howdy Reichmuth and other staff volunteers worked on a 400-square-foot community solar greenhouse through rain and cold. The greenhouse is a symbol, a rallying point. It will have a

Ecotope, a Northwest community-oriented, non-profit research group, has its headquarters in a lovely Victorian mansion in Seattle (far left). It also operates an organic farm in the countryside, some forty miles away, where the first stave of a large greenhouse is being erected by its members (upper left).

parabolic solar reflector to heat a 32-foot-long, 6-foot-wide, and 4-foot-deep fish tank. Here, Prag-tree plans to raise *Tilapia Mozambiqua,* a herbivorous fish that is low on the overall food chain. Fish farming is only part of the link in the chain of the life-support system that Ecotope envisions—embracing food, shelter, tools, energy, communication. PRAG members began raising the fish at the group's Seattle base (in a tank in the basement) with success.

Food and energy are at the heart of Ecotope's activities and research. Vegetables, raised at the farm, are sold to food co-ops in the Seattle area. Pragtree gets its hot water from a thermosiphon collector on its farmhouse and is installing two Jacobs wind generators for its electrical power. Jointly with *Rain,* Ecotope bought a third Jacobs

to display at energy workshops that are an important part of their educational program. In weekend workshops in Washington, California, and Wyoming, Ken Smith and Lee Johnson have now taught over five hundred people how to build their own solar collectors to heat hot water for use in the home. The workshops are attended by county energy assistants, community action groups, and private citizens, who are shown how to do the carpentry and plumbing and put together the collectors for under $100. Once instructed, these people can then pass on the know-how to others in their own localities. As Johnson reported in *Rain,* December 1975 issue, "It became delightfully obvious that a rapid transition toward a solar society will be not only much easier than many people would believe, but it will be one of the most popu-

lar and politically acceptable events between now and the year 2000. People want to relate to peaceful technologies they can understand, to sciences basically grounded in human experience—sunrise, sunset, and the changing seasons—and to energy systems of which they have no fear." The reaction of people when they see the hot water solar collectors built before their eyes is always the same: "Why, this is so simple! Why aren't there more of these around?" "Then," Johnson continues, "they realize there are now a dozen collectors when there were none and there are now at least five hundred people who know how to go beyond those twelve devices. And they see that a great many things are possible under the sun."

Pragtree publishes a monthly newsletter of its own, called *Tilth*, which is full of news on the alternative agriculture movement in the Cascade region. It's a sort of *Farmers Almanac* with information that ranges from a lead article on land trusts to a discussion of solar-heated greenhouses to ads for a crop of soybeans.

Ecotope also acts as professional consultant to business, government, and public utilities. One of the projects they helped plan and put into action was the construction of a methane gas plant at the State Prison Honor Farm in Monroe, Washington. This plant, with a 100,000-gallon capacity to process the manure of three hundred fifty dairy cows, is the largest bio-gas plant in operation since World War II. It is expected to produce nearly 2 billion Btu's of methane per year with a return of about $10,000 a year in savings of fuel oil and ammoniated nitrogen fertilizer. Ecotope is seeking funds from the Bioconversion Division of ERDA. The money is needed to complete a break-in phase of the system and also to produce an operator's training manual. But, according to Evan Brown, "ERDA seems more interested in giving grants to large companies and universities for theoretical studies than in supporting the pioneer projects already under way."

Sharing space with Ecotope staff members and a group of teenagers that the community adopted, is Nicholas Licate, who published the useful *Guide to Seattle* in 1975. The book exemplifies the group's involvement with the community as a whole. Politics, however, isn't Ecotope's thrust. Ken Smith, especially, shies away from making extravagant claims unless they can be supported with a body of achievement. "When we have something to say, we will say it," he stated flatly. It will be worth listening to.

Ecotope has a program of workshops they sponsor to show the public how to make flat-plate solar collectors (far left). So far, the group has taught over 500 people how to build a solar collector for under $100 to heat domestic hot water.

One of Ecotope's most ambitious projects is a methane gas plant (left), designed for the State Prison Honor Farm in Monroe, Washington. With a 100,000 gallon capacity, the plant is the largest bio-gas plant in operation since World War II.

Farallones Institute

"We are beginning to train people to make their own place in society."

Farallones Institute, like Ecotope in Seattle, has a city-country axis, an urban center in Berkeley, California, and a farm in Occidental, California. It is a nonprofit research and educational group devoted to "whole life systems." That, according to its president, Sim Van der Ryn, who is also the state architect of California, means living, working, sharing, and learning to create a small-scale life system in balance with nature.

The Berkeley center, where Farallones started in October 1974, has headquarters in a donated Victorian house in a run-down industrial-residential section by the railroad tracks. "We wanted to get right in there," says Tom Javits, the center's manager, "and to show by example what we could do to improve the city environment. We put wood chips on the sidewalk because they are nicer to walk on than concrete and they also provide a good medium for microorganisms. We planted alfalfa in place of grass because it is self-fertilizing and doesn't have to be cut. These mulberry

The community of Berkeley, California, has a verdant garden in its midst, thanks to Farallones Institute. This non-profit research group, headed by California state architect Sim Van der Ryn, also shares its produce with the community by selling it at an urban version of a farmer's market. Headquarters are in an old townhouse (above) given the Institute by a private donor.

trees in front of the house aren't just for show. The leaves feed silkworms whose silk we use as fiber for clothing. And we feed the pupae, as a good source of protein, to the chickens. As bait for our flytraps, we collect dog manure (which cleans the streets) and then mix it with molasses. Then we feed the flies to our chickens. Our whole approach to gardening is based on low-labor, interrelated systems."

The most visible feature of the Farallones Institute is its flourishing garden in downtown Berkeley. The plot, measuring 50 square feet in the backyard, supplies more food than the house members can eat, Javits says—fava beans, beets, lettuce, cabbage, broccoli, kale, carrots, and radishes. He added that each week they were getting thirty eggs from the chickens and 5 pounds of meat from the rabbits. They have also planted apricot, pear, apple, plum, and lemon trees, all dwarf varieties and some espaliered on the fence. "It takes little labor," he claimed. "We only grow what's appropriate for urban people."

At first, the neighbors were indifferent to the garden in their midst. Now they are beginning to respond positively by fixing up their own gardens and taking better care of the general area.

During its first year, the center's dozen or so members, which include three or four students, carried out a complete remodeling of the rundown house. Farallones' staff includes people with varied skills, in biology, architecture, engineering, and agriculture, who contribute to the research and educational programs. Three student-residents are studying the biophysical systems of the house, and one institute member, Charles O'Laughlin, is working on how to recycle nutrients and organic matter to the soil through composting and excreta management. The house is also a classroom for courses geared to low-income people, on growing food in the city, using solar-heating systems, and other energy-saving topics. Mobile units also travel the state and local agriculture fairs with similar informative sessions and demonstrations.

Even on Sunday, the Farallones farm north of Berkeley in pastoral Occidental is a beehive of activity. Members, including the institute's president, Van der Ryn, work the 80-acre ranch of rolling hills, redwoods, vineyards, and orchards in the hot sun. "In the spring of 1975, we started with five members to set the cornerstone for the basic life-support system—a garden, water supply, privy, kitchen, and wash area," says Karen Katz. "Our first priority was to remodel and expand the existing buildings, which also taught us basic carpentry and plumbing." Buildings were remodeled for the office, library, and indoor meeting space; the dilapidated barn was patched up to house a cow and several dozen chickens. A bread box solar hot water collector, built largely of salvaged materials, heats the water for the shower house.

A terraced hillside, covering 1 acre, was cultivated with vegetables and other unrelated plants for biological pest control. The group has also experimented with drip irrigation, using buried water cans, and improved mulching. They tested different vegetables, fruits, herbs, and flowers to see which would thrive best in the region. A similar approach was applied to the livestock, which included a Guernsey cow, four pigs (raised on garbage), rounded out with the chickens, rabbits, and a few goats.

Another project involves an effort to upgrade gray water from sinks and showers in a specially dug pond where a wind-powered generator "cleans" the water by circulating air through it. Nutrient-absorbing water plants further purify the water, which then will be used for irrigation.

"We aren't seeking quick, easy solutions," say Tom Javits of the urban group and David Katz, the rural director. The Farallones effort is a slow process of easing into the existing social structure. "We are beginning to train people to make their own place in society," Javits adds. "As we move ahead, neighbors respond. If enough people do this kind of thing, it will transform the country through a growing awareness."

Ouroboros

"Each region needs its own architectural style to work with, rather than against, nature."

Ouroboros is an experiment in autonomous living sponsored by the University of Minnesota architectural and engineering department. It was named for a mythical serpent that survived and regenerated by eating its own wastes and tail. It began in the winter of 1973, when Dennis Holloway, a professor of architecture, gave one hundred sixty students a project, to design an experimental, energy-saving house. The three award-winning designs were incorporated into a prototypical energy-saving house. The student class then went on to build that house on a site forty minutes from the university's main campus, at its Rosemount Research Center. The 2,000-square-foot house was not meant to be a finished habitat but rather a teaching laboratory for the university students and the public. The university contributed the land, and local businesses and the power companies donated materials and funds.

The house combines old ideas about shelter with modern technology. The north side is a sloping sod roof (like those used for centuries in Scandinavia), while the south facade is a bank of steeply pitched solar collectors, angled at 60 degrees. In winter, the snow mantle that settles on the sod roof is excellent natural insulation. Other design features to reduce winter heat loss and increase sum-

The facade of Ouroboros South (left) stands in striking contrast to the north-facing back (below). This prototype of an energy-conscious house grew out of a design competition at the University of Minnesota school of architecture and engineering. The winning designs were incorporated into one plan, which the students then built themselves. In the photograph the greenhouse for the building is in an advanced stage of construction.

mer cooling are semiunderground construction, extra insulation, and a tepee-like vent in the roof. The solar collectors supply both space heat and hot water. A wind generator is being completed to supply electricity for lights and cooking.

Professor Holloway, who left his architectural practice in New York to teach in the Midwest, encouraged the students to conserve the small energy increments that add up over the course of a day's living. At Ouroboros, the bathrooms have jet spray nozzles in sink and shower, a Clivus Multrum toilet connected to a compost system, a Japanese-style soaking tub (originally a cedar beer barrel that soaks four adults at a time)—all

designed to cut down on water usage. "Ouroboros is an ongoing experiment in low-impact self-sufficiency," says Holloway.

To the students and the faculty, Ouroboros South (as the house is called) was a smash success. The next question was, would it work in the city? Holloway, with Thomas Kelley, who was then president of Urban Laboratory, Inc., a neighborhood-improvement consulting firm, and who is now the St. Paul City administrator, got a HUD grant and for $1 bought an older house on Laurel Avenue in a 30-square-block Model Cities urban renewal area in downtown St. Paul. Thus was born Ouroboros East. Teams of university stu-

Several principles combine to give the Ouroboros project its form. The low, north side allows cold winter winds (dark arrows) to glance off the sod-covered roof. Air intake vents near the ground do let in breezes (broken arrows) for summer cooling, however. The house is partially buried in the ground to keep the interiors warm through the earth's natural insulating properties. On the south facade, the solar collectors are steeply tilted to face into the sun. Below them, a greenhouse is designed to supply the house with additional heat as well as with a place to grow vegetables.

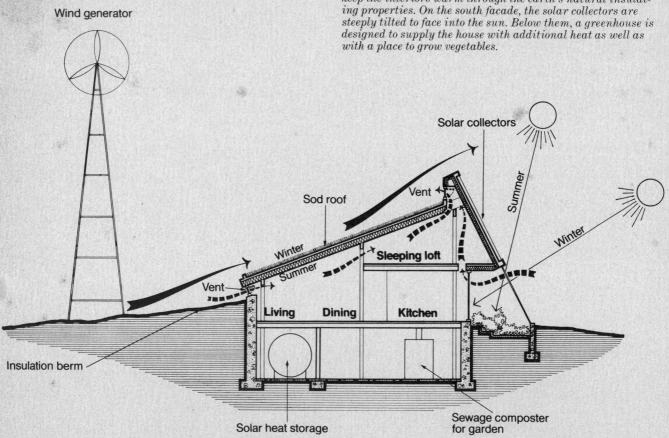

Wind generator

Solar collectors

Vent

Sod roof

Sleeping loft

Summer

Winter

Winter

Summer

Vent

Living   Dining   Kitchen

Insulation berm

Solar heat storage

Sewage composter for garden

dents from the architectural and engineering departments are retrofitting the building for solar energy.

The Laurel Avenue house was ideal because its south-facing back roof could accommodate solar collectors without noticeably changing the house from the street side. Holloway and Kelley met with the local community leaders to ease their new environmental ideas into the neighborhood. Kelley also got a special ordinance change in the St. Paul building codes to legalize the use of solar collectors.

After remodeling was completed, the building became, in Holloway's words, "a kind of *Whole Earth Catalog* of what can be done to conserve energy in an old house." Insulating the shell was paramount. The house was stripped of its interior fittings, and four different types of insulation were employed: fiberglass batts, urea foam, formaldehyde foam, and loose fill (made of shredded newspapers). Some of the windows were boarded over; the rest were given insulating glass. Like Ouroboros South, this house has been equipped with a Clivus Multrum toilet and Japanese tub.

Three radically different solar collectors are being tested for their relative efficiency at Ouroboros East: (l) the standard flat plate system based on the work of Harry Thomason of Wash-

In plan, Ouroboros South is basically a combined kitchen, living and dining area, with a small, enclosed bathroom on the ground level. Two decks open off the house. One is located beside the entry and vestibule on the east side and another opens through sliding glass doors on the south, or front. The dotted lines inside the house perimeter indicate the second story loft area. The dotted lines on the exterior of the house indicate the slope of the trapezoidal roof.

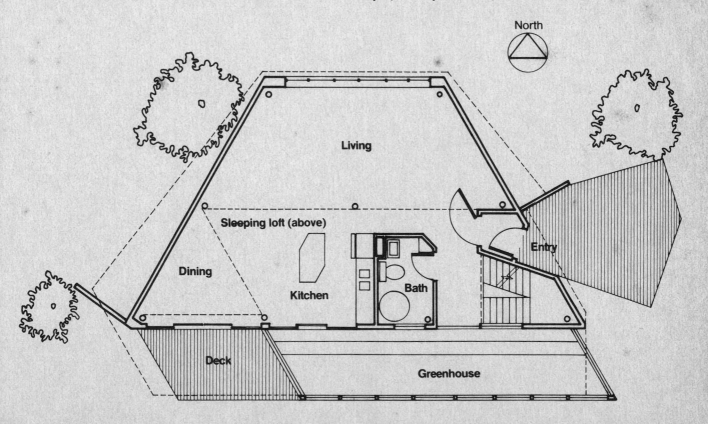

189

After the success of Ouroboros South, the students at the University of Minnesota decided to try their hands at an urban example of energy-saving design. They bought an older building in St. Paul (below) from the city for $1.00 and are now retrofitting it for solar heating (right).

ington, D.C.; (2) a prototype of a 1,200-square-foot internal flow, steel-sandwich collector developed at the University of Minnesota; and (3) a totally different concept, a parabolic collector. The combination provides all of the house's hot water and about 70 percent of its winter heat, the backup electric furnace supplying the rest.

Live-in students monitor the systems of Ouroboros East and run an educational center. Students are also testing standard household appliances there to determine how they might be improved. They are working on such projects as insulating the refrigerator, redesigning appliances to use less energy, and studying how pots and pans can cook with less heat. They are also building a greenhouse and a 1,200-square-foot garden behind the house, which they hope will provide one-third of their produce.

"One lesson already learned from the Ouroboros experiment," Holloway said, "is that each climatic region needs its own architectural style to work with, rather than against, nature." What works in Minnesota does not hold true for Georgia. "We have found here that the winter sky is so overcast that instead of the standard 60-degree angle for the collector, we get better results by mounting it closer to vertical," he added.

Primarily, though, Ouroboros is a learning center. "It is a place where people of all kinds can see energy conservation systems and then use the workshop to build their own," said Holloway. "Since most of us live and work in cities, we have to begin to develop our new technologies right now and right in the middle of our urban centers," Kelley adds. "That's what Ouroboros East is designed to do."

519 East Eleventh Street

"I love looking down the street and knowing that I helped put it back together. I feel I have a real stake in my community."

A Manhattan tenement building on East Eleventh Street, in the middle of a ghetto inhabited by a scrambled mix of Blacks, Puerto Ricans, Poles, and Jews, is the site of the first operating solar collector in New York. On March 15, 1976, it pumped its first solar-heated water from the rooftop collectors down to the newly installed storage tank in the basement. It is a triumph and an anomaly, a humanistic dream that bypassed the city's government bureaucracy, fiscal crisis, and public apathy. The building, number 519, used to be owned by one of the neighborhood's worst slumlords; it was the scene of fifteen fires in one month and was slated for demolition. Today it is owned cooperatively by eleven people, nearly all under thirty-five years of age, who reclaimed it by "sweat equity." 519 East Eleventh Street is Manhattan's showcase prototype of urban homesteading. And it is the first of three more buildings on the block slated for rehabilitation.

"519," as it is now popularly known, is the result of the efforts of a new breed of young political activists working with the ghetto community. "This was not a visionary kind of thing," says Travis Price, one of the building's brain-trust advisors, "it was a last resort, a bare necessity for those who lived here. They had no place to go, they had to make it work; they couldn't afford to move to the suburbs." Most of the co-op residents, like Roberto Nazario and Santiago Gonzales, lived on or near the block. Others, like Travis Price and Michael Freedberg, were volunteers who walked into the Lower East Side sensing a need for their engineering skills and seeing their involvement as a moral-political stance. Others, like Tom Grayson, Everett Barber, Charles Copeland, David Norris, and graduate students like Alva Tabor, who did his M.I.T. thesis on the Eleventh Street experi-

"Sweat equity" by members of a ghetto community resuscitated an old tenement in Manhattan (far left). It is the site of the first operating solar collectors in New York City. The building's co-owners, who are also its construction crew, stand on the roof in front of the banks of collectors. Inside (left), they are seen putting in insulation during renovation.

ence, also volunteered their technical and manual assistance. Grayson, in fact, not only designed the solar heating system, but also supervised its installation.

"519" was conceived in 1974 by three of the co-op's original members—Michael Freedberg, who came to New York from New Haven, Connecticut; Roberto "Rabbit" Nazario (who got his nickname as a child dodging cops); and Hal Landy. Travis Price joined the project six months later, having just returned from Santa Fe, New Mexico, where he had been with the Sun Mountain Design group. (He left, he says, because the Southwest solar community was becoming too smug and complacent and the cities offered a greater challenge for energy conservation. As one of his Sun Belt cohorts, Wayne Nichols, put it, "We're out here creating the new world while you're going back East to clean up the mess we left behind.")

The core group formed a corporation and got a municipal loan of $177,000, bought "519" for $1,800, and started a "sweat equity" program, campaigning on street corners to get block residents involved. The Community Services Administration gave a grant of $43,000 to convert the building to solar-heated water. After the building was gutted down to the exterior walls and a few rafters, about $11,000 was spent for high-grade insulation. Another $15,000 went for the solar equipment, consisting of 600 square feet of collectors that rise in three banks on the roof of the building. The frames of the collectors, painted in vivid colors of red, yellow, blue, and green, can be seen from the Empire State Building. "It's the first colored solar collector system in the country," Travis Price quipped.

The thing that makes "519" unique is that it is an example of grass-roots conservation. Preserving the building was the first goal. Insulating it with full-batt insulation plus rigid insulation over studs, storm windows, and good sealants resulted in a 60-percent reduction of the building's heat loss. In the basement a 550-gallon tank was installed to store the solar-heated water. The solar hot water system saves another 20 percent in total energy needs.

"Sweat equity," a term for investing in labor what you can't give in funds to build equity in a place to live, contributed nearly all of the building's installation expenses. The shareholder-tenants—some single and some married, about 60 percent of them Puerto Rican—are the board members of the 519 East Eleventh Street Housing Development Corporation, and also the building's painters, spacklers, floor layers, garbagemen, paralegal professionals, and lobbyists. They paid themselves $3 an hour to work a thirty-two-hour week; one eight-hour day each week, representing each worker's investment in his own apartment, was donated free.

By the time the sweat-equity owners moved into the renovated building, they had worked on it for a year and a half. None had any previous construction experience, although now most are

skilled workers and can sell their skills in the marketplace. Their motives for becoming involved were as simple as those of Joe B. Barnes, a twenty-four-year-old Antiguan bachelor who quit his job to join "519" because, as he remarked matter-of-factly, "everyone deserves a decent place to live." Karen Berman, a twenty-one-year-old Brooklynite, recalls, "I don't know how we did it. There were no windows and no heat, and we were working nine hours a day in the middle of winter when the snow drifted into the building. I'll never regret it, though. We're like a family now; you don't always love each other, but you're in it together."

The project transformed the street from a hardcore poverty area, where car stripping was a cottage industry, into a concerned neighborhood. "Eleventh Street between Avenue A and Avenue B was lawless," says Rabbit Nazario (who is now known informally as "the Mayor of the Lower East Side"). "Cars left parked for less than fifteen minutes were broken into and stripped." Junkies accosted pedestrians and hawked 'hot' merchandise. The block is now an ongoing scene of construction activity—three additional tenements are currently under renovation.

Michael Freedberg, the house intellectual, sees the project as seminal in the fight to save the cities. "In the whole history of urban renewal and Model Cities," he says, "the government programs have done nothing to stop the deterioration. What was missing was bringing the people into it, showing them how to do it, giving them an opportunity to accomplish what government money could not. We're doing it here—and I really get off on that."

Graffiti on a wall on East Eleventh Street spell out the severity of Manhattan's housing crisis. The owners of 519 (below), who rehabilitated the building with their own labor, smile with pride at their accomplishment. Behind them, the spire of the Empire State Building is just visible on the horizon.

As for the solar system, Freedberg observed that it was inevitable. "Sweat equity, rehabbing tenements, and solar energy all go together. You can't isolate one way of thinking from the others. But solar technology is only the tip of the iceberg. It isn't the whole answer to energy conservation. You've got to go into the neighborhood, into every building, and show the tenants how to caulk the windows, replace the washers in the faucets, fix the faulty valves, and install money-saving insulation. That's what conserving energy is really all about."

With the apathy and economic wars fought and almost won, "519" has become a model for other homesteading efforts in poverty areas, particularly where landlords abandon buildings because of escalating maintenance costs. "We have created an energy task force," Travis Price says. "Banks and businesses are coming to us to see what we've done. It's a third-world model for low-income housing programs that others can imitate." Partly as a result of "519"'s success, the federal government has granted $3 million to the newly formed National Center for Appropriate Technology, which sponsors and gives advice to similar urban projects.

But to Santiago Gonzales, thirty-five, married, an actor who hopes to start a community theater when the work on Eleventh Street is finally over, the benefits are more on a gut level. "I love looking down the street and knowing that I helped put it back together. I feel I have a real stake in my community."

Organizations and Groups to Contact for Further Information

American Institute of Aeronautics and Astronomy, Milwaukee Student Branch, 3228 North 26th Street, Milwaukee, WI 53206. Information on the public benefits that have come from the space exploration programs, including information on solar and fuel cells.

American Society of Heating, Refrigerating and Air-conditioning Engineers, Inc. (ASHRAE), 346 West 47 Street, New York, NY 10017. Provides data for proposed energy standards.

Boulder Solar Energy Society, P.O. Box 3431, Boulder, CO 80303. Information on all solar technologies.

California, University of, Department of Environment and Horticulture, Davis, CA 95616. Jonathon Hammond, Coordinator. Information on solar technologies and building code changes related to solar energy and energy conservation.

Center for California Public Affairs, 226 West Foothill Boulevard, Claremont, CA 91711. Information on alternate energy sources.

Center for Environment and Man, 275 Windsor Street, Hartford, CT 06120. A group that conducts energy conservation research.

Center for Research, Acts of Man, 4025 Chestnut Street, Philadelphia, PA 19104. Social considerations regarding energy use and conservation, also, general information on all solar energy technologies.

Center for Science in the Public Interest, 1785 Massachusetts Avenue, Washington DC 20036. Jim Sullivan, Co-director. Issues consumer guides to solar and other alternate technology systems.

Citizens for Energy Conservation and Solar Development, P.O. Box 49173, Los Angeles, CA 90049. A citizens' action group that provides advice and information regarding its activities.

Delaware, University of, Institute for Energy Conversion, Newark, DE 19711. Involved in all aspects of solar research.

Ecology Action Education Institute, Box 3895, Modesto, CA 95352. Publishes original research on solar energy.

Energy Policy Project, 1776 Massachusetts Avenue, N.W., Washington, DC 20036. Publishes original research on solar energy.

ERDA (Energy Research and Development Administration), 1800 G Street, N.W., Washington, DC 20545. Federal agency that incorporates the Atomic Energy Commission (AEC), National Science Foundation (NSF), the Environmental Protection Agency (EPA), and the Department of the Interior.

Energy Research Corporation, 6 East Valerio, Santa Barbara, CA 93101. Group maintains an energy data bank.

Environmental Action Coalition, Educational Materials Program, 235 East 49th Street, New York, NY 10017. Maintains an energy data bank.

Environmental Action Foundation, 720 DuPont Circle Building, Washington, DC 20036. A citizens' action group.

Environmental Action of Colorado, 2239 East Colfax, Denver, CO 80206. A total information clearing house on solar technologies.

Environmental Energy Foundation, Room 1001, 1200 Edgewater Drive, Lakewood, OH 44107. Group conducts solar research and gives out information on it.

Environmental Information Center, 124 East 39th Street, New York, NY 10016. Group maintains a reference and retrieval service covering environmental affairs.

Farallones Institute, 15290 Coleman Valley Road, Occidental, CA 95465. Information on solar water heating and also on totally integrated life support systems.

Florida, University of, Department of Solar Energy/Energy Conversion, Gainesville, FL 92611. Erich H. Farber, Director. College conducts research on solar energy.

Friends of the Earth, 529 Commercial Street, San Francisco, CA 94111. Citizens' environmental action group.

Friends Research Center, Environmental Studies, 308 Hilton Avenue, Catonsville, MD 21228. Information about the political considerations of solar energy as well as information about solar technologies in general.

HUD (Department of Housing and Urban Development), Energy Affairs, Room 10230, 451 7th Street, S.W., Washington, DC 20410. Information on the financial considerations of solar energy applications.

Illinois, University of, Advanced Computer Center, Urbana, IL 61801. College maintains an energy data bank.

Inform, 25 Broad Street, New York, NY 10004. Group distributes information on energy conservation.

Institute for Local Self-Reliance, 1717 18th Street, N.W., Washington, DC 20009. A citizens' environmental action group.

International Solar Energy Society, American Section, c/o Florida Solar Energy Center, 3000 State Road, 401 Cape Canaveral, FL 32920. An international organization of scientists and laymen devoted to furthering the use of solar energy.

Lama Foundation, P.O. Box 444, San Cristobal,

NM 87564. The foundation engages in original solar research and will share the results.

Legislative Energy Commission, New York State, Room 718, L.O.B., Albany, NY 12207. James I. Monroe, Scientific Advisor. Distributes information regarding solar energy legislation.

Library of Congress, Division of Science and Technology, Washington, DC 20540. Will provide solar energy data.

MIT (Massachusetts Institute of Technology), Architecture School, 3-407 MIT 77, Massachusetts Avenue, Cambridge, MA 02139. W.E. Heronemus, Professor. Carries out research on wind energy and on ocean gradient thermal systems.

McGill University, MacDonald College, Brace Research Institute, Ste. Anne de Bellevue 800, Quebec H9X 3MI, Canada. Distributes pamphlets and information on all solar technologies.

Metropolitan Ecology Workshop, 74 Joy Street, Boston, MA 02114. Distributes information on all solar technologies.

Minnesota, University of, Department of Architecture and Landscape Architecture, 110 Architecture Building, Minneapolis, MN 55455. Dennis R. Holloway, Assistant Professor. Distributes information on their solar projects, such as Ouroboros.

Mother Earth News, Inc., P.O. Box 70, Hendersonville, NC 28739. Distributes information on grass roots use of solar energy, bio-conversion and methane production.

Mountain Area Domestic Solar Energy Technical Consortium, R.D. 2, Box 274, Evergreen, CO 80439. Gives out information on all solar energy technologies.

NASA (National Aeronautics and Space Administration), Lewis Research Center, Solar Systems

Section, 21000 Brookpark Road, Cleveland, OH 44135. Conducts research on space heating and cooling.

National Academy of Sciences, Building Research Advisory Board, 2101 Constitution Avenue, N.W., Washington, DC 20418. Distributes information on solar space heating and cooling.

National Association of Home Builders (NAHB), Research Foundation, Inc., P.O. Box 1627, Rockville, MD 20850. Publish technical books and conduct energy conservation research for the builder and developer.

National Council for the Public Assessment of Technology, 1757 S Street, N.W., Washington, DC 20009. Byron Kennard, Director. Provides technical assistance for local citizen groups.

National Science Foundation, Advanced Energy Research and Technologies, Washington, DC 20550. Distributes information on all solar technologies.

New Alchemy Institute, East Coast Division, P.O. Box 432, Woods Hole, MA 02543; West Coast Division, Box 376, Pescadero, CA 94040. Gives out information on its alternate energy experiments and integrated life support systems.

New England Sierra Club, 14 Beacon Street, Boston, MA 02108. Distributes information on solar technology and energy conservation.

New England Solar Energy Association, P.O. Box 121, Townsend, VT 05353. Distributes news on regional solar energy activity.

New Mexico Solar Energy Association, 6021 Canyon Road, Santa Fe, NM 87501. Keith Haggard, President. Distributes information on all aspects of energy conservation and solar technologies.

New York State Council on Architecture, 810 Seventh Avenue, New York, NY 10019. Gives out information on solar energy design in new construction.

Open Northwest Information Network, 608 19th Avenue E, Seattle, WA 98112. Publishes periodicals for the layman on alternate energy sources.

Ozark Access Center Inc., 55 Spring Street, Box 506, Eureka Springs, AR 72632. Publishes periodicals for the layman on alternate energy sources.

Portola Institute, Energy Primer, 558 Santa Cruz Avenue, Menlo Park, CA 94025. Publishes lay and technical books on alternate energy technologies.

Rand Corporation, 1700 Main Street, Santa Monica, CA 90406. Conducts research on energy conservation, publishes statistics.

REDE (Research and Design Institute), P.O. Box 307, Providence, RI 02901. Distributes and conducts research on alternate energy technologies.

Resources for the Future, Energy Research and Technology, 1755 Massachusetts Avenue, N.W., Washington, DC 20036. Distributes information about the foundations that provide grants and funds for alternate energy research.

Solar Energy Research and Information Center, 1001 Connecticut Avenue, N.W., Washington, DC 20036. Distributes information about solar energy industries and manufacturers.

Solar Energy Society of America, 2780 Sepula Boulevard, Torrance, CA 90510. Publishes lay and technical periodicals.

Solar Sustenance Project Inc., Bill and Susan Yanda, Route 1, Box 107 AA, Santa Fe, NM 87501.

Southern California, University of, WESRAC, 809 West 34th Street, Los Angeles, CA 90007. Provides information on all solar technologies.

Stanford Research Institute, Energy Technology, 333 Ravenswood Avenue, Menlo Park, CA 94025. Publishes original research material.

Sun Publishing Company, P.O. Box 4383, Albuquerque, NM 87106. Publishes lay and technical periodicals.

Synergy Peoples' Pages, P.O. Box AH, Stanford, CA 94305. Publishes books for the layman; write for a list.

Total Environmental Action, Box 47, Harrisville, NH 03450. Publishes brochures on energy-conserving housing design.

U.S. Department of Agriculture, Independence Avenue, S.W., Washington, DC 20250. Charles Beer, Director, Extension Service. Distributes information about its solar water heating research.

U.S. Weather Bureau, National Weather Record Center, Federal Building, Asheville, NC 28801. Distributes statistical weather data for all the United States for the past fifty years.

Product Source List
Manufacturers of Solar-related Hardware for Residential Use

Arkla Industries, Inc., 400 E. Capitol, Little Rock, AR 72203.
Solar aluminum and copper flat plate liquid-type collectors.

Corning Glass Works, Lighting Products Division, Corning, NY 14830.
A variation of solar collectors, utilizing glass cylinders mounted in a metal frame.

CSI Solar Systems Division, 12400 49th St., N., St. Petersburg, FL 33732.
Solar copper flat plate liquid-type collectors for water heating.

E.I. Du Pont de Nemours, Inc., Wilmington, DE 19898.
Transparent plastic glazing for solar collectors: brand name is "Tedlar PVF."

E&K Service Co., 16824 74th Ave., N.E., Bothell, WA 98011.
Solar liquid-type collectors, thermostatically controlled pumps, heat exchangers, heat storage tanks.

Edmund Scientific Co., 300 Edscorp Bldg., Barrington, NJ 08007.
Sells plans for Harry Thomason-designed solar homes.

Energex Corp., 481 Tropicana Rd., Las Vegas, NV 89109.
Markets ten models of liquid-type copper solar collectors.

Energy Systems Inc., 634 Crest Drive, El Cajon, CA 92021.
Solar aluminum and copper flat plate collectors.

Environmental Energies, Inc., 21243 Grand River, Detroit, MI 48219.
"Solarator" domestic hot water heater, solar flat plate collectors, wind-energy products.

FAFCO, Inc., 138 Jefferson Dr., Menlo Park, CA 94025.
ABS plastic solar collectors for swimming pools.

Free Heat, P.O. Box 8934, Boston, MA 02114.
Solar heat systems including flat plate liquid-type collectors, pumps, storage beds.

Fun & Frolic, Inc., P.O. Box 277, Madison Heights, MI 48071.
"Solarator" PVC plastic collectors for swimming pools or do-it-yourself space heating.

Garden Way Labs, P.O. Box 66, Charlotte, VT 05445. Solar aluminum collector panels for domestic hot water.

Grumman Aerospace Corp., Energy Systems Dept., Plant 30, Bethpage, NY 11714.
"Sunstream" solar hot water systems, wind power products.

Helio Associates, Inc., 8230 E. Broadway, Tucson, AZ 85710.
Sells plans for air-type collectors for space heating.

Helio-Dynamics Inc., 518 S. Van Ness Ave., Los Angeles, CA 90020.
Solar domestic hot water systems.

Heliotec, Inc., 33 Edinboro St., Boston, MA 02160.
Manufacturers of transparent insulating glazing materials.

Henry Mathew, RT. 3, Box 768, Coos Bay, OR 97420.
Plans for Mathew's own solar collector system (see page 40).

Hitachi America Ltd., 437 Madison Ave., New York, NY 10022.
"Hi-Heater" is the brand name of this solar domestic hot water heater.

International Rectifier, Semiconductor Div., 233 Kansas St., El Segundo, CA 90245.
Manufacturers of photovoltaic cells for converting the sun's energy directly to electricity. Also publish a $2 handbook for experimenters.

International Solarthermics Corp., Box 397, Nederland, CO 80466.
"Sungazer," a preassembled free-standing air-type solar furnace for retrofitting.

Isothermics, P.O. Box 86, Augusta, NJ 07822.
Secondary heat recovery mechanisms.

Kalwall Corp., 1111 Candia Rd., Manchester, NH 03105.
Solar air-type collector. Also manufacturers of plastic glazing for collectors.

Libbey Owens Ford Co., 811 Madison Ave., Toledo, OH 43695.
Solar collector components.

Löf Brothers Solar Appliances, P.O. Box 10594, Denver, CO 80210.
Absorptive surfacing materials.

Megatherm Corp., Taunton Ave., East Providence, RI 02914.
Chemical thermal storage mediums.

Paul Mueller Co., P.O. Box 828, Springfield, MO 65801.
"Temp-Plate" stainless-steel heat-transfer surfacing material.

Niagara Blower Co., 405 Lexington Ave., New York, NY 10017.
Solar hardware for refrigeration and dehumidification.

Olin Corp., Brass Group, Roll-Bond Products, East Alton, IL 62024.
Flat plate heat-exchanger panels.

Physical Industries Corp., Solar Division, P.O. Box 357, Lakeside, CA 92040.
Solar liquid-type heat panels, steam-fueled engines.

PPG Industries, Inc., 1 Gateway Center, Pittsburgh, PA 15222.
Solar glass components, flat plate water-type collectors.

Raypak Inc., 31111 Agoura Rd., Thousand Oaks, CA 91360.
Liquid-type flat plate collectors; also solar swimming pool heaters.

Revere Copper & Brass Inc., P.O. Box 151, Rome, NY 13440.
Solar flat plate copper liquid-type collectors.

Reynolds Metal Co., 2315 Dominguez St., Torrance, CA 90508.
Solar aluminum water-type flat plate collectors.

Rho-Sigma, 5108 Melvin Ave., Tarzana, CA 91356.
Thermostats for solar heating systems.

Fred Rice Productions Inc., 6313 Peach Ave., Van Nuys, CA 91401.
Solar water heaters; solar-energy appliances such as clocks, radios, etc. Also importers of "SAV" solar water heater from Australia.

Rohm & Haas, Plastics Dept., Independence Mall West, Philadelphia, PA 19105.
Plexiglas for collector covers.

Skytherm Processes and Engineering, 2424 Wilshire Blvd., Los Angeles, CA 90057.
Plans and specifications for Harold Hay's "thermal pond" solar heating and cooling system (see page 28).

Solar Energy Products Co., Avon Lake, OH 44012.
Manufacturers of a solar air-type collector for drying of harvested crops.

Solar Energy Research Center, P.O. Box 17776, San Diego, CA 92117.
"Solapak" collectors and hot water storage tanks imported from Beasley Industries, Ltd., Australia.

Solar Energy Research Corp., Rt. 4, Box 268, Longmont, CO 80501.
Solar heat and storage systems.

Solar Energy Systems Inc., 70 S. Chapel St., Newark, DE 19711.
Low-cost photovoltaic systems to supply solar electricity.

Solarex Corp., 1335 Piccard Dr., Rockville, MD 20850.
Producers of silicon solar cells.

Solaron Corp., 4850 Olive St., Denver CO 80022.
Solar pioneer George Löf (page 32) is a Vice President of this manufacturer of complete air- and water-type solar heating systems.

Solar Power Corp., 186 Forbes Rd., Braintree, MA 02184.
Low-cost photovoltaic systems.

Solar Power Corp., 930 Clocktower Pky., Village Square, New Port Richey, FL 33552.
Flat plate liquid-type copper collectors for domestic hot water.

Solarsystems Inc., 1802 Dennis Dr., Tyler, TX 75701.
Aluminum flat plate collectors.

Solergy, 150 Green St., San Francisco, CA 94111.
Manufacturers of a solar collector utilizing spiral and parabolic surfaces.

Sol-Therm Corp., 7 W. 14th St., New York, NY 10011.
Distributors of "Amcor" liquid-type flat plate collector imported from Israel.

Spectrolab, division of Textron Solar Power Systems, 12484 Gladstone Ave., Sylmar, CA 91342.
Photovoltaic cells for solar electricity.

Suhay Enterprises, 1501 E. Windsor Rd., Glendale, CA 91205.
Plans for do-it-yourself domestic hot water and swimming pool heaters.

Sundu Co., 3319 Keys Lane, Anaheim, CA 92804.
Plastic ABS hot water heaters.

Sunearth Co., Inc., Box 99, Milford Square, PA 18935.
Manufacturers of water-type flat plate collectors for space heating.

Sunsource, 9606 Santa Monica Blvd., Beverly Hills, CA 90210.
"Miramit" solar collectors from Israel for both space and hot water heating.

Sunwater Co., 1112 Pioneer Way, El Cajon, CA 92020.
Aluminum and copper flat plate water-type collectors.

Sunworks, Inc., 669 Boston Post Rd., Guilford, CT 06437.
Distributors of copper water-type flat plate collectors by Enthon, Inc., New Haven, CT.

Thomason Solar Homes Inc., 6802 Walker Mill, S.E., Washington, DC 20027.
Building plans for Harry E. Thomason's solar-heated houses.

Tranter Inc., 735 E. Hazel St., Lansing, MI 48909.
Water-type flat plate collectors, platecoil components for heat storage tanks.

Unitspan Architectural Systems Inc., 6606 Variel, Canoga Park, CA 91303.
Prefabricated modular aluminum flat plate collectors.

Zomeworks, Inc., Box 712, Albuquerque, NM 87103.
Steve Baer (page 44) produces his designs for "skylid" water heaters, bead wall construction, and solar hot water heaters.

Manufacturers of Wind-related Hardware

American Energy Alternatives Inc., P.O. Box 905, Boulder, CO 80302.
Wind turbine, photovoltaic 6- to12-volt systems, solar water heaters.

American Wind Turbine, P.O. Box 446, St. Cloud, FL 32769.
Wind generators.

Dempster Industries, Inc., P.O. Box 848, Beatrice, NB 68310.
"Annu-Oiled" steel windmill for pumping water.

Dyna Technology Inc., P.O. Box 3263, Sioux City, IA 51102.
Producers of 200-watt, 12-volt "Winchargers."

Enertech, P.O. Box 420, Norwich, VT 05055.
Distributors of Australian "Dunlite," Swiss "Elektro," U.S. "Windco" wind generators and accessories.

Garden Way Laboratories, P.O. Box 66, Charlotte, VT 05445.
Home-sized wind-energy systems.

Pennwalt Corp., Automatic Power Div., P.O. Box 18738, Houston, TX 77023.
Distributors of "Aerowatt" wind generators imported from France.

Sencenbaugh Wind Electric, P.O. Box 11174, Palo Alto, CA 94306.
Solar electric power generators.

Sensenich Corp., P.O. Box 1168, Lancaster, PA 17604.
Wood propellers for wind generators.

Shaw Pump Co., 9660 E. Rush St., South El Monte, CA 91733.
Windmills for pumping water.

Solar Wind, P.O. Box 7, East Holden, ME 04429.
Distributors of "Wincharger" by Dyna Technology.

Windworks, Box 329, Rt. 3, Mukwonago, WI 53149.
Wind generators and accessories.

Zephyr Wind Dynamo, P.O. Box 241, Brunswick, ME 04011.
Patented windmill.

Glossary

adobe. Sun-dried bricks for building, made of clay indigenous to desert regions of the Southwest.

air-to-rock. A solar heating system comprised of flat plate collectors which circulate sun-heated air. This air is then fed through ducts into a bin of rocks where it transfers its heat to the rocks to be stored for later use.

alternating current (AC). Electrical current in which the flow of electrons reverses at regular intervals; in the United States, the alternating frequency is 60 cycles per second.

ambient temperature. The prevailing temperature of the air surrounding an area.

ampere (amp). The intensity of electric current flowing in a given circuit.

auxiliary heat source. A supplementary way to provide heat to a space when the primary source is not sufficient.

balloon framing. The system of building currently used for most house construction. It consists of a structural frame composed of vertical wood members, such as posts or columns, and horizontal 2 × 4-inch studs, placed regularly at 16-inch intervals. These horizontal members support the roof joists and rafters. The part of the roof frame that is flat is a joist, the sloping members are called rafters. The whole rests upon the subfloor of plywood or planking, laid over floor joists and finally, upon the building's foundation, either concrete footings or concrete block.

battery. A device to store electrical energy for later use.

batts or *batt insulation.* Loose material such as glass wool or fiberglass that is sandwiched between flexible paper and aluminum foil. This forms a long bag that fits between the rafters, joists or studs. This type of insulation is sold in long rolls, which can be cut off as needed.

beam. A major horizontal structural member of a building, which supports minor structural members such as joists.

bearing wall. A supporting wall; or one which supports the upper stories and the roof.

belvedere. A tower or high extension on the top of a building. Originally, from the Italian, meaning "beautiful view."

berm. A man-made earth mound or hill generally piled against the north side of a house for natural insulation.

boiler. A furnace that heats water to produce steam for space heating.

brushes (of a wind generator). Spring-loaded flanges made of carbon that brush against the rotor, thereby collecting the electricity produced in the generator.

Btu (British thermal unit). The amount of heat necessary to raise the temperature of a pound of water one degree Fahrenheit.

bung. The cap or stopper that seals a barrel.

clerestory. A portion of an interior rising above adjacent rooflines and having windows positioned to allow for ventilation and lighting.

Clivus Multrum toilet. Toilet manufactured by A.B. Clivus of Sweden that processes effluent by aerobic composting. Sewage and kitchen wastes are composted together with grass, leaves, earth and peat mould to yield a humus that is removed at yearly intervals from a refuge chamber. During this resting period, the compost pile is aerated through pipes buried in the chamber. The temperatures inside the chamber rise as high as 150 degrees, or high enough to destroy harmful bacteria.

closed loop. A solar heating system in which the pipes, circulating liquid from the collectors to the storage vehicle, form a closed, continuous loop. The medium used in this system is generally a mix of water and antifreeze. It is used where cold winters could cause water in the solar collectors to freeze overnight and damage the system.

column. A vertical or upright structural member of a building. Columns can be made of various materials such as wood, steel or concrete.

compressor. A motor-driven device that compresses gases.

condensation. Water droplets formed on a cold surface from contact with warmer, moisture-laden air.

condenser. A component of a heating and cooling system in which a fluid, such as Freon, undergoes a change from gas to liquid. In the process, heat is generated. (See also *heat pump.*)

conduction. The transmission of heat by contact between a cold surface and a warmer one.

convection. The transmission of heat by moving masses of air. Air convection follows the natural law that warm air rises while cooler air falls.

diffused sky radiation. Indirect sunlight or sunlight obscured by clouds as opposed to direct beam sunlight.

direct current (DC). Electrical current which flows in one direction only.

double glazing. Windows which have two sheets of glass with an airspace in between. Also called insulating glass, or Thermopane, because the airspace reduces the amount of heat lost by conduction through the windows.

duct. A chamber or tube through which air flows.

effluent. Discharged organic wastes, suspended in liquid.

energy load. The amount of energy it takes to accomplish a task. Applied to a house, it is the term used to define the total amount of energy expended for all purposes, such as space heating and cooling, heating water, running appliances and lighting.

energy storage. The ability to convert energy into other forms, such as heat or a chemical reaction, so that it can be retrieved for later use.

evaporator. A component of a heating and cooling system in which a working fluid undergoes a change from liquid to gas, extracting heat and producing a cooling effect. It operates in a manner directly opposite to that of a condenser and both are part of a heat pump, air conditioner and refrigerating system.

exhaust fan. A fan in the wall or ceiling that draws out, or exhausts, stale air.

facade. The frontal view of a building.

fission. The release of large amounts of energy by the splitting of an atomic nucleus.

fixed glass. A glass panel used like a window, except that it cannot be opened.

flashing. Sheet metal or other waterproof material used to prevent water from getting through joints where two exterior surfaces meet, such as the joining of the roof and chimney.

flat plate collector. A device for gathering the sun's heat. It consists of a shallow metal box with a glass or plastic transparent lid, where either air or liquid is circulated through the cavity of the box. In the liquid-type collector the back plate of the metal box is fitted with tubes through which the liquid circulates. The collectors are angled to face the sun so that the heat medium, be it air or liquid, is heated to temperatures averaging 120 degrees. The medium, if it is water, is then piped down to a large water tank for storage and, if air, to a bin of rocks.

flue. The exhaust channel through which gas and fumes are released from a building.

footing. A concrete base used beneath foundation walls and columns to distribute evenly the building's weight load to the ground.

fossil fuel. Organic compounds formed by the decay of matter by heat and pressure over millions of years. When burned, the compounds release energy. The fossil fuels most frequently used by man are coal, oil and natural gas.

foundation wall. A heavy masonry or concrete wall, designed to support the weight load of a building, as well as to resist the pressure of the ground from the sides.

Freon. A highly stable (or inert) gas that does not combine readily with other chemical elements and, for that purpose, is used in heat pumps and refrigeration systems.

fuel. Any substance that can be expended to produce heat or power.

furling. Stopping the rotors of a wind generator so that they cannot turn.

fusion (nuclear). The release of energy by fusing two atomic nuclei.

geothermal. Heat radiating outward from the earth; from the Greek *geo*, meaning "earth," and *thermal*, meaning "heat."

generator. A machine for producing electricity. (See also *wind generator.*)

governor (of a wind generator). A device that automatically controls the speed of the rotors by changing their angle. In a high wind, the governor turns the blades into the wind, called *feathering*, to prevent damage to the machine.

heat exchanger. A device used to transfer heat from one medium to another.

heat gain. The increase of heat in a space resulting from direct solar radiation and from heat given off by lights, equipment, machinery and people.

heat loss. The depletion of heat in a space resulting from loss through the walls, windows and roof.

heat pump. A reversible heating and cooling mechanism that can produce additional usable heat from the amount stored. It operates via a compressor and an evaporator, causing a liquid, such as Freon, to expand and contract. A heat pump works by circulating Freon in a closed cycle through two sets of coils. In one half of the cycle, a motor powers a compressor, which raises the pressure of the Freon and causes it to condense in the condenser to liquid form, creating heat. In the other half of the cycle, the liquid passes to the coils of the evaporator, where a lower pressure causes it to evaporate, expand or to revert to a gas, creating cool air. In the process, either the heat from the compressor cycle or the cold from the evaporator cycle can be drawn off, either to heat or cool a given space. The most familiar form of heat pump is that of a standard refrigerator.

heat sink. A large body or mass capable of absorbing and storing heat over a period of time. Concrete, adobe, other masonry walls and also large barrels or tanks of water are effective heat sinks.

hogan. An earth-covered lodge used by the Navahos.

humus. Decaying organic matter, either animal or plant material, which is an essential element of all fertile soil.

HVAC. An abbreviation for heating, ventilating and air conditioning.

hydroelectric plant. An electrical power plant using the kinetic energy of water to produce electricity by a turbine generator.

hydronic heating. A hot water heating system.

hydroponic gardening. Growing vegetables and plants in a predominantly liquid medium as opposed to a soil medium.

incident sunlight. Direct sunlight, as opposed to diffused sunlight.

infiltration. The flow of air into and out of a building through the openings of doors and windows, and by penetration through cracks and crevices of doors, windows and the building shell itself.

insolation. Incident solar radiation or the amount of solar radiation striking a surface.

insulation. Filler material placed within the wall, floor or ceiling of a building to reduce the loss of warm or cold air from within a building to the outside.

inverter. A device for converting direct current (DC) to alternating current (AC).

joist. One of a series of evenly spaced horizontal structural beams usually made of lumber, steel or concrete, for supporting floors and ceilings.

Jøtul. One of several models of cast-iron wood-burning stoves imported from Scandinavia that burns logs in an enclosed heat chamber. The Scandinavian stove is much more efficient than the ordinary fireplace because a single log lasts four times as long and radiates all of its heat into the room. In the ordinary fireplace, most of the heat is lost up the chimney and only a fraction actually warms the room.

kilowatt. A unit of power equaling 1000 watts.

kilowatt-hour (kwh). A unit of energy equaling the consumption of 1000 watts in one hour.

louver. An opening with slanted overlapping slats allowing the circulation of air. Louvers are often used for air flow in rooms requiring visual privacy.

manifold. A special duct or pipe that has a single intake valve and several outlet valves used for joining other pipes to it. A manifold distributes a single flow of air into several ducts.

masonry. Anything built of brick, stone or concrete block.

methane. A colorless, odorless, flammable gas produced by the decomposition of organic matter. It is a major component of natural gas.

parabolic collector. A device for collecting the sun's energy that utilizes a bowl or disk-shaped reflector. The reflector, which is often mirrored, concentrates the radiation, producing extremely high temperatures, as much as 3,000 degrees Fahrenheit.

peak load. The maximum demand of an appliance, a building or community for energy.

photovoltaic cell. A solar or photoelectric cell. This special cell generates electricity directly by exposure to the sun's rays.

plasterboard. See *Sheetrock.*

plate glass. A quarter-inch thick window glass.

plenum. A chamber in which the air pressure is greater than that of the surrounding air.

polyethylene. A thin, transparent sheet of plastic used for moistureproofing floors and walls and also as a covering for greenhouses.

polystyrene. Panels of a foamlike plastic used for house insulation.

polyurethane. Plastic that can be applied as a foam and sprayed into the recesses of the frame of a building, where it expands and forms an insulating barrier.

radiant heat. The heat gained in a house or room by heat emitted from large, sun-warmed surfaces, such as walls or floors.

radiation. The emission of energy or heat waves. Solar radiation is the emission of rays by the sun; thick, exterior walls of a building can also radiate the heat they have absorbed from the sun all day back into the interior spaces at night.

radiator. A series of pipes containing steam or hot water that is designed to emit heat to the surrounding area. The pipes can also circulate cold water to cool a given area.

recovered energy. Reusing heat or energy that would otherwise be lost. For instance, heated air from a clothes dryer can be vented back into the house or routed to an energy storage bin, such as the rock beds of a solar heating system.

rectifier. A device that converts alternating current (AC) into direct current (DC).

recycle. To recover and reuse materials and resources.

retrofit. A catchword meaning the installation of solar collectors and other hardware onto an existing house to convert it for solar heating.

sheathing. Material, such as plywood or planks, fastened to the wall studs or rafters of the roof of a building to stiffen and strengthen the structure. It then provides the base for attaching the exterior finishing material.

Sheetrock. Plasterboard. A rigid panel of gypsum and paper nailed to the studs that forms the interior wall surface. In recent years, plasterboard has replaced the more costly and more difficult to apply, hand-finished plaster.

skylid. An opening skylight, the latter being permanently affixed. The skylid is a window in the roof that can be opened.

skylight. A window placed in the roof of a building.

solar collector. A device used to gather and accumulate the sun's heat or solar radiation. The most common type for home use is the flat plate solar collector.

solar hardware. All of the devices and equipment needed to build a solar heating and domestic hot water system. This includes the flat plate collectors, the pipes, gauges, valves, circulating pumps, fans and blowers, as well as the storage facility, which can be water drums or rock bins.

space heating. The heating of a building or a room interior.

stucco. A mixture of cement, lime, sand, and water that hardens to become both a waterproof and decorative surface material.

studs. Evenly spaced upright supports that form the skeleton for walls and partitions of a building.

tensile structure. A structure that is formed by the stress or stiffening of its material. A tent is a good example of a tensile structure. The term also applies to structures created by equilateral tension, such as a geodesic dome.

thermal lag. The time that it takes for the inside air temperature of the house to heat up or cool to that of the surrounding outside temperature. If the house is particularly well insulated or constructed with a thick masonry shell, the thermal lag is greatly prolonged. This time lag accounts for the natural heating and air conditioning in many passively-designed solar-heated buildings.

thermal mass. The quantity or bulk of a heat-absorbing material, such as stone, brick, concrete or adobe.

thermal transmission. The passage of heat through a material.

thermodynamics. The science of heat-induced motion or mechanical activity. Specifically, the natural laws pertaining to heat energy.

thermosiphon water collector. A flat plate collector that circulates water (through the collector) by means of natural convection. The water storage tank is placed above the collector. Cool water leaves the tank and flows into the collector where it is heated by the sun. As the water is warmed it rises naturally and returns to the tank.

Trombe wall. A passive solar heating system devised by Felix Trombe and Jacques Michel that combines the solar collector and heat storage in a one, south-facing wall unit. They experimented with the design in houses in the Pyrenees and in central France. The system consists of a thick concrete wall painted black on its outer face. A sheet (or sheets) of glass are placed in front of this wall with an airspace between. Air from the rooms of the building passes through openings at the foot of the wall, entering the airspace where it is heated by the sun. As it warms, the air rises up the air cavity by natural convection. It passes back into the building interior again through a second series of openings at the top of the wall. In order to arrest the flow of warm air into the building in summer, the openings in the wall are blocked by shutters.

vapor barrier. A thin sheet of plastic or layer of felt that prevents the penetration of moisture into a building.

vent. A pipe or duct that permits gases or air to escape to the outside.

ventilation. Outside air that is purposely allowed to enter an interior space to cool or freshen it.

volt. The unit of pressure in an electric circuit.

voltage regulator. A device that controls the amount of electricity produced by the generator to prevent overcharging and damaging an electrical system.

watt. The unit of rate at which work is done in an electrical circuit, equal to the rate of flow (amperes) multiplied by the pressure (volts).

wind energy. The energy of air motion over the earth's surface caused by the sun's heating of the atmosphere.

wind generator. Any one of a number of devices used to convert wind energy into electricity.

wind generator rotors. The blades or propellers of a wind machine.

Further Reading
Helpful Books and Brochures

Prices and dates have been supplied wherever possible. However in cases where the books and brochures are privately published, this information was not readily available.

Alternative Natural Energy Sources in Building Design. A. J. Davis and R. P. Shubert, Passive Energy Systems Research Consulting, P.O. Box 499, Blacksburg, VA 24060.

Build Your Own Greenhouse: How to Construct, Equip, and Maintain It. Charles D. Neal, Chilton Press, 201 King of Prussia Rd., Radnor, PA 19089. 1975. ($9.95)

Composting Privy: Technical Bulletin No. 1, Sim Van der Ryn, Farallones Institute, 15290 Coleman Valley Rd., Occidental, CA ($1.00) A basic guide.

Cooperative Community Development: A Blueprint for Our Future. Joe Falk, ed., Future Associates, P.O. Box 912, Shawnee Mission, KS 66201. ($2.95) Organizing a neighborhood, block by block, real estate acquisition, co-op purchasing, creating jobs and volunteer labor bank, organizing a credit union, working with lending institutions. It's all portrayed in loving detail, so it's obvious the author has had lots of experience.

Design Criteria for Solar-Heated Buildings. Everett M. Barber and Donald Watson, AIA, Sunworks Inc., P.O. Box 1004, New Haven, CT 06508. 1975. ($10.00) Appendix outlines how to figure percentage of space heating that a given solar heating system can provide.

Design with Climate, Victor V. Olgyay, Princeton University Press, Princeton, NJ 08540. 1963. ($25.00) Important early book being rediscovered by architects.

Direct Use of the Sun's Energy. Farrington Daniels, Yale University Press, 302 Temple St., New Haven, CT 06511. 1964. ($12.50) Ballantine paperback, 1974. ($1.95) Fairly technical classic introduction to solar energy.

Do's and Dont's of Methane, The. Al Rutan, Juicy Press, 1809 Portland Ave., Minneapolis, MN 55404. ($3.00)

Electrical Power from the Wind. Henry Clews, Solar Wind Publication, P.O. Box 7, East Holding, ME 04429. ($2.00) Small but information-packed brochure from the wind expert.

Energy: A Guide to Organizations and Information Resources in the U.S., Center for California Public Affairs, Publications Dept., 226 W. Foothill Blvd., Claremont, CA 91711.

Energy, Environment and Building. P. Steadman, Cambridge University Press, 32 E. 57th St., New York, NY 10022. 1975. ($5.95, paperback) Excellent overview of state of the art. Excerpts from most major sources on conservation. Exhaustive bibliographies.

Energy Miser's Manual, The. William H. Morrell, Grist Mill Publishing, Eliot, ME 03903. 1974. ($2.25)

Energy Primer: Solar, Wind, Water and Biofuels. Richard Merrill et al., eds., Whole Earth Truck Store, 558 Santa Cruz Ave., Menlo Park, CA 94025. 1975. ($5.50) Comprehensive review of renewable energy systems. Lists books, plans, kits, where to buy; has graphs, etc.

Handbook of Homemade Power, Editors, *Mother Earth News,* Mother Earth News, P.O. Box 70, Hendersonville, NC 28739. Excerpts of articles on solar, wind, methane systems.

Handmade Greenhouse: From Windowsill to Backyard, The. Richard Nicholls, Running Press, 38 S. 19th St., Philadelphia, PA 19103. 1975. ($4.95, paperback) Detailed plans, introduction to tools and building techniques, light and plant culture.

Harnessing the Sun to Heat Your House. John H. Keyes, Morgan & Morgan, 145 Palisades St., Dobbs Ferry, NY 10522. 1975. ($2.95)

Homebuilt Wind Generated Electricity Handbook, The. Michael Hackleman, Earthmind, Saugus, CA 91350. ($7.50) Using renovated wind generators, especially Jacobs and Winchargers.

Hot Water: Solar Water Heaters and Stack Coil Heating Systems. S. Morgans et al., 350 E. Mountain Dr., Santa Barbara, CA 93108. ($2.00) Information on flat plate collectors for home use; information on open- and closed-loop systems.

How to Build a Solar Water Heater. Brace Research Institute, MacDonald College of McGill University, Ste. Anne de Bellevue 800, Quebec H9X 3M1, Canada. ($1.00) Detailed instructions for building a thermosiphon-type corrugated plate collector.

How to Challenge Your Local Electric Utility: A Citizen's Guide to the Power Industry. Richard Morgan and Sandy Jerabek, Environmental Action Foundation, 720 DuPont Circle Building, Washington, DC 20036.

How to Construct a Cheap Wind Machine for Pumping Water. A. Bodek, Brace Research Institute, MacDonald College of McGill University, Ste. Anne de Bellevue 800, Quebec H9X 3M1, Canada. ($1.25) Bulletin with basic instructions.

Kilowatt Counter: A Consumer's Guide to Energy Concepts, Quantities and Uses. Gil Friend and D. Morris, Alternative Sources of Energy (ASE), Rt. 2, Box 90A, Milaca, MN 56352. ($2.00)

Lifestyle Index. Albert Fritsch, Center for Science in the Public Interest, 1779 Church St., N.W., Washington, DC 20036. 1974. ($1.50) Charts tell the amount of energy Americans use and compare it to world averages—includes everything from hair

dryers to food. Excellent for consciousness raising.

Living Lightly: Energy Conservation in Housing. Tom Bender, Office of Energy Research and Planning, 185 S.E. 13th, Salem, OR 97201. ($1.50) Ideas on the need for change in building and lifestyles.

Low-Cost, Energy-Efficient Shelters for the Owner and Builder. Eugene Eccli, ed., Rodale Press, Emmaus, PA 18049. ($5.95) Design principles for building sensibly at a price, including simple winterizing projects up to full-scale design and construction to build or renovate a house.

Methane Digesters for Fuel Gas and Fertilizer. Richard Merrill and L. John Fry, New Alchemy Institute, Box 376, Pescadero, CA 94060. ($3.00) Information from the experts.

Natural Energy Workbook. Peter Clark, Visual Purple, Box 979, Berkeley, CA 94701.

New Low-Cost Sources of Energy for the Home. Peter Clegg, Garden Way Publishing, Charlotte, VT 05445. 1975. ($5.95, paperback) Excellent practical information on how and where to build and how much to pay for water, wind, solar power, methane digesters, wood heating. Catalog included.

Other Homes and Garbage: Designs for Self-Sufficient Living. Jim Leckie et al., eds., Sierra Club Books, 530 Bush Street, San Francisco, CA 94108. 1975. ($9.95, paperback) Assortment of well-illustrated chapters by environmental engineers on solar energy, putting waste to work, improving water supplies, building low-energy-consuming structures, using wind and water power.

Power from the Wind. Palmer C. Putnam, Van Nostrand Reinhold Co., 450 W. 33rd St., New York, NY 10001. 1948. ($9.95) Readable account of the experimental windmill at Grandpa's Knob. Contains excellent drawings, charts, and graphs as a basis for expanded research.

Practical Sun Power. W. H. Rankins and D. A. Wilson, Lorien House Publisher, P.O. Box 1112, Black Mountain, NC 28711. ($4.00) Good how-to manual for a variety of simply constructed solar-energy devices made from easily available materials.

Producing Your Own Power: How to Make Nature's Energy Sources Work for You. Carol H. Stoner, ed., Vintage Books, Random House, 201 E. 50th St., New York, NY 10022. 1975. ($3.95, paperback) Sections by several experts on self-sufficient living, including Henry Clews on wind generating and J. B. DeKorne on the survival greenhouse.

Radical Technology. Godfrey Boyle and Peter Harper, eds., Pantheon Books, Random House, 201 E. 50th St., New York, NY 10022. 1975. ($5.95) First published in the United Kingdom as *The Energy Primer*, this is a kind of *Whole Earth Catalog* on alternate technology.

Save Energy, Save Money. Eugene Eccli, Community Services Administration, 1200 19th St., N.W., Washington, DC. 20506

Simplified Wind Power Systems for Experimenters. Jack Park, Helion, Box 4301, Sylmar, CA 91342. ($6.00) One of the best introductions to wind generator systems.

Solar Energy and Shelter Design. Bruce Anderson, Total Environmental Action (TEA), Church Hill, Harrisville, NH 03450. ($7.00)

Solar Energy Directory. Carolyn Pesko, Ann Arbor Science Publishers, P.O. Box 1425, Ann Arbor, MI 48106. ($20.00) A comprehensive listing of solar activities, activists. 600+ pages.

Solar Energy Handbook. P. A. Fleck, ed., Time-Wise Publications, P.O. Box 4140, Pasadena, CA 91106. ($4.45) Conversions, equivalents, and definitions needed by experimenters.

Solar Energy Home Design in Four Climates. Total Environmental Action (TEA), Church Hill, Harrisville, NH 03450. ($12.75) Analysis of passive systems for four major climates in the U.S. An excellent book.

Solar-Heated Houses: For New England and Other North Temperate Climates. Massdesign, Architects and Planners, Inc., 18 Brattle St., Cambridge, MA 02138. ($7.50)

Spectrum: An Alternative Technology Equipment Directory. Alternate Sources of Energy (ASE), Rt. 2, Box 90A, Milaca, MN 56352. ($2.00) Catalog of tools and processes for small-scale use of solar, wind, water, and other forms of energy.

Strategy for Energy Conservation. (Proposed Energy Conservation and Solar Utilization Ordinance for the City of Davis, California) Jonathan Hammond et al., Living Systems Inc., Rt. 1, Box 170, Winters, CA. ($5.00)

Sun Angle Calculator. Libby-Owens Ford Co., Attn: Corporate Affairs, Mdse., 811 Madison Ave., Toledo, OH 43695. ($5.00) Circular slide rule for locating the position of the sun and angle of incidence.

Sun/Earth: How to Use Solar and Climatic Energies Today. Richard L. Crowther, AIA, Crowther/Solar Group, 310 Steele St., Denver, CO 80206. ($12.50) 1976. Large format, beautifully illustrated and eminently readable survey of architecture and its relation to the natural environment.

Sunspots. Steve Baer, Zomeworks Corp., P.O. Box 712, Albuquerque, NM 87103. ($3.00) 1975. Odyssey of ten years' experience with small-scale solar-energy devices.

Survival Greenhouse, The. Jim DeKorne, Walden Foundation, P.O. Box 5, El Rito, NM 87530. 1975. ($7.50, paperback) Top-notch description of trials and errors encountered in a couple's self-sufficiency program with description of their solar-powered hydroponic greenhouse.

350 Ways to Save Energy (and Money) in Your Home and Car. Henry R. Spies et al., Crown Publishers, 419 Park Ave. S., New York, NY 10016. 1974. ($5.95, paperback)

To Live With the Earth: A New Lifestyle. Project Survival, P.O. Box 13372, Portland, OR 97208. A book about alternate living in Oregon by a group who have begun the weaning process themselves.

Wastewater Engineering: Treatment, Collection, Disposal. Metcalf and Eddy, McGraw-Hill Book Co., 1221 Avenue of the Americas, New York, NY 10020. 1972. ($23.50) Best textbook on subject.

Whole Earth Catalog, Whole Earth Epilog, Co-Evolution Quarterly. P.O. Box 428, Sausalito, CA 94965. Continuing update by the granddaddy of access catalogs.

Wind and Solar Thermal Combinations for Space Heating. Wind Power Group, University of Massachusetts, Amherst, MA 01002. (free)

Wind and Windspinners. Michael A. Hackleman and David W. House, Peace Press, 3828 Willat Ave., Culver City, CA 90230. 1974. ($7.50) Copies also available from Earthmind, Josel, Saugus, CA 91350. Comprehensive information on wind systems. Excellent for S-rotor builders.

Wind Power. P. E. Syverson and J. G. Symons, Ph.D., Box 233, Mankato, MN 56001. 1973. ($3.00) Concise description of wind energy for individual use, glossary, references, list of consultants, information on backup systems and assessing one's electric needs.

Periodicals

Alternative Sources of Energy. Rt. 2, Box 90A, Milaca, MN 56353. ($5.00/yr, quarterly) Only periodical in the country devoted exclusively to information on small-scale renewable energy systems. Issue No. 17, 1975 ($2.00), is an excellent directory with 436 product reviews.

Co-Evolution Quarterly. Box 428, Sausalito, CA 94965. ($8.00/yr, quarterly) *Whole Earth Catalog* group's periodical.

Energy Action News and Views. Citizens for Energy Conservation and Solar Development, P.O. Box 49173, Los Angeles, CA 90049. (donation) Citizens' action newsletter.

Energy Reporter. Federal Energy Administration, Washington, DC 20461. (free) Miscellaneous tidbits from the FEA; a citizens' newsletter of propaganda.

New England Solar Energy Newsletter. New England Solar Energy Association, P.O. Box 121, Townshend, VT 05353. ($5.00/yr, monthly) News on activity in New England, where utility bills are skyrocketing.

Not Man Apart. Friends of The Earth, 529 Commercial St., San Francisco, CA 94111. ($10.00/yr, bimonthly)

Rain: Journal of Appropriate Technology. 2270 N.W. Irving St., Portland, OR 97210. ($10.00/yr, ten issues) Lively magazine devoted to news of environmental action groups.

Self-Reliance Newsletter. Institute for Local Self-Reliance, 1717 18th St., N.W., Washington, DC 20009. ($6.00/yr, bimonthly)

Solar Age. Rt. 515, Box 288, Vernon, NJ 07462. ($20.00/yr, monthly) Publication devoted to monthly news about solar energy developments in a fast burgeoning field.

Solar Energy Intelligence Report. c/o Business Publishers, Inc., P.O. Box 1067, Silver Spring, MD 20910. ($40.00/six months) Best description of current government activity, grants, and legislation.

Solar Engineering. 8435 North Stemmons Freeway, Suite 880, Dallas, TX 75247. ($10.00/yr, monthly) Reports on all aspects of solar energy, activity, trade news, and new products.

Tilth Newsletter. Box 2382, Olympia, WA 98507. ($5.00/yr) Down-home newsletter is an excellent source for alternative technology in agriculture.

Undercurrents. Undercurrents Ltd., 275 Finchley Rd., London N.W. 36 LY, England. ($6.50/yr, bimonthly) Excellent political/technical descriptions of the alternative technology movement in England, where the British live closer to the edge.

Wind Power Digest. Rt. 2, Box 489, Bristol, IN 46507. Access to wind equipment, designs, periodicals.

About the Authors

NORMA SKURKA is Design Editor of *The New York Times Magazine* and has contributed weekly stories on residential and industrial design for the past seven years. She has also been an editor with *House Beautiful* and *Interior Design* magazines. She is the author of the books *Underground Interiors* (Quadrangle, 1970) and *The New York Times Book of Interior Design and Decoration* (Quadrangle, 1976).

JON NAAR is a widely published photographer specializing in design and environmental subjects. Mr. Naar's work appears regularly in *The New York Times Magazine*, *Fortune*, *Elle*, and other publications in both the United States and Europe. He is the photographer of *The Faith of Graffiti* (Praeger, 1974). Mr. Naar is also a writer, and co-author of *Living in One Room* (Random House, 1976).